Eagle Seamanship

A Manual for Square-Rigger Sailing

REVISED BY
Paul M. Regan,
Lieutenant Commander, U.S. Coast Guard

Paul H. Johnson
Librarian, U.S. Coast Guard Academy

Naval Institute Press
Annapolis, Maryland

Library of Congress Catalog No. 77-95011
ISBN 0-87021-166-8

Produced under the auspices of the
United States Coast Guard Academy

Cover design based on a photograph
by BM1 J. R. Stone, USCG

Printed in the United States of America

Contents

Foreword

The *Eagle* is a cadet-operated training vessel. As is not the case in all training vessels, cadets do all the jobs aboard the *Eagle* necessary for the ship's day-to-day operation: from mess cook to officer of the deck; from engineroom oiler to master-at-arms; from boatswain's mate of the watch to engineering watch officer. There is a small cadre of enlisted personnel to provide technical know-how in such areas as engineering and communication; however, there are only four rated boatswain's mates aboard to provide rigging expertise. To the extent that the *Eagle* is sailed smartly and routines are executed in a seamanlike manner, the upper-class cadets can take pride in their achievements of training and leading the under-class cadets aboard. Conversely, if the *Eagle* is not handled smartly and if procedures and routines are haphazard, the upper-class cadets must bear the lion's share of the responsibility. That is but one aspect of this truly unique vessel.

The miles of standing and running rigging and the 21,350 square feet of sail demand of the cadets the development of proficiency in marlinspike seamanship and generate an appreciation for the forces created by wind and sea beyond that which one might gain aboard a screw-driven vessel. But the *Eagle*'s true value as a training vessel lies in the demands she places upon cadets to perform involved maneuvers under trying circumstances. In no other environment and on no other ship do cadets have the opportunity to direct the activities of large numbers of people in situations that require command presence, an ability to monitor and evaluate a particular evolution, and the necessity to use mental flexibility. It is frequently necessary to alter the intended timing or command to meet changing circumstances—all in a manner that projects confidence in an environment where the effects of howling wind, rain, darkness, and pounding seas must be addressed and, where possible, employed to reach the end desired.

Aboard the *Eagle,* large numbers of cadets can frequently be assigned leadership roles under demanding conditions, which enables them to evaluate their own shortcomings or successes. They then have the opportunity to apply, during future evolutions, the knowledge gained through their own observations and through the advice given by reviewing officers. The sailing environment additionally provides opportunities for officer supervisors to form judgments concerning an individual cadet's ability to function effectively in conditions of stress. Such evaluations are important to the maintenance of an officer corps which has gained an international reputation for consisting of skilled seamen whose duties often demand that they operate in a hostile marine environment in order to save the lives of hapless seamen endangered by hurricane-force conditions.

Those of you who are about to embark aboard the *Eagle* can rest assured that her personnel are not only ready to test your mettle, but are poised to assist you in developing competence as seamen. To take advantage of your future training, you must join the *Eagle* with more than familiarity with this text. The description of the various evolutions must be read and reread until you are able to reason through and recite the numerous commands associated with each evolution. Only then will you be prepared to gain fully from your square-rigger experience—an experience that will prepare you, as can no other, effectively to deal with your future career challenges.

PAUL A. WELLING
Commander, U. S. Coast Guard
Commanding Officer

October 1978

Acknowledgments

With the exception of some diagrams, the glossary, and a small part of the text, this edition of *Eagle Seamanship* is completely new. I must give credit, however, to W. I. Norton, the author of the first edition, for collating a large quantity of complicated information into a form readily understood by cadets, and for providing a firm foundation on which the present edition could be based. Likewise, I must thank the U.S. Coast Guard Academy Foundation for permission to use material from the first edition.

Chapter One, the history of the *Eagle*, was written for the first edition by Robert Dixon, assistant librarian at the Coast Guard Academy. It has been revised and updated, on the basis of new-found material, by Paul Johnson, the head librarian at the academy.

Invaluable advice and assistance in writing this edition were provided by CWO Richard (Red) Shannon, USCG, sailing master of the *Eagle*, CWO Howard Hudgins, USCG, engineering officer of the *Eagle*, and Lieutenant Robert Winters, USCG, of the Coast Guard Academy's Professional Studies Department. These gentlemen made numerous suggestions for improving the text and eliminating ambiguities. Finally, I would like to thank Commander Paul A. Welling, USCG, commanding officer of the *Eagle*, for acting as coordinator with the publisher and carefully checking proof of the text. Of course, any errors remaining are my own.

PAUL M. REGAN

1. History of the *Eagles*

Today's square-rigged barque *Eagle* is the seventh Coast Guard vessel to bear that name. The *Eagle*s span many years and many changes.

The Coast Guard traces its history to ten revenue cutters authorized by the first Congress in 1790 at the instigation of Alexander Hamilton, the first Secretary of the Treasury. These ten cutters (so called for their English rig) operated as the Revenue Marine in collecting customs duties and enforcing the revenue laws.

The first *Eagle* was stationed in Savannah, Georgia under the command of Captain John Howell. Howell's *Eagle* served as the Georgia cutter from 1792 until 1798 or 1799 when she was replaced by a captured French vessel renamed *Bee*. The United States had entered into an undeclared naval war with France in 1796. This war with the nation's former ally intensified when some sixty to eighty French privateers based at Guadeloupe in the West Indies continued to molest American ships. In May 1798, the United States Navy was formed to meet such threats, and hastily acquired fifty-four vessels, of which eight were revenue cutters. This cooperation with the new Navy established a custom that has been observed in all wars down through the years and remains today.

The war with France was a strange war, for it depended on sailing skill and bluff as much as on gunfire. Some fifty war vessels of the United States were divided into four squadrons, but the Secretary of the Navy, Benjamin Stoddert, insisted on a strategy where each vessel sailed an independent course. With some sixty to eighty French ships often chasing an equal number of American merchant ships and naval vessels, it was not unusual for American ships to speak to each other. In this way, prize vessels on both sides were often retaken. Though some ships never met the enemy; the relatively fast revenue cutters captured more than their share.

One of these valiant little cutters was a brig named *Eagle*. Designed by Josiah Fox and built at Philadelphia in 1798 by William and Abra Brown, the 187-ton vessel was fifty-eight feet along her keel, twenty feet across her beam, with a nine-foot hold and a crew of seventy, including fourteen marines. She mounted fourteen 6-pounders through her gun ports.

The captain of this second *Eagle* was Hugh George Campbell of South Carolina, a demanding but efficient master of his ship. He was not afraid to challenge the Secretary of the Navy, who deemed the *Eagle* ready for sea before he did. Secretary Stoddert ordered the ship to join the 20-gun *Montezuma,* commanded by Captain Alexander Murray, and two other vessels at Norfolk. They were to cruise the West Indies to protect American merchantmen. However, the *Montezuma* sailed without the *Eagle*. Piqued at Campbell's delay, Secretary Stoddert ordered him to cruise the coasts of Georgia and South Carolina. Campbell's later record in the West Indies raised the Secretary's low opinion of him to such heights that in July 1799, Campbell was commissioned a Navy master commandant. In October 1800, he was made a captain, which was at that time two grades higher than a captain of the Revenue Service.

In November 1800, Captain Campbell was selected to command the 28-gun frigate *General Greene* in place of Captain Christopher R. Perry, the father of the commodore, who had been relieved of his command for three months by court-martial. Captain Campbell was replaced on the *Eagle* by Lieutenant M. Simmones Bunbury of Maryland. During the Barbary Wars, Campbell was raised to the command of the frigates *Constellation* and *Constitution*, and from 1805 to 1807 was commodore of the Mediterranean Squadron.

In the West Indies from 1798 to 1800, the *Eagle* was one of the most successful ships, first in the squadron of Stephen Decatur, Sr., later in that of Commodore John Barry. In all, the *Eagle* captured five French armed vessels. On two other occasions, she assisted the ships *Delaware* and *Baltimore* in taking prizes. In addition, several American merchant vessels captured by the French were retaken by the *Eagle*. One of her best captures was the schooner *Bon Pere,* which was renamed *Bee* and used by the American forces.

After Lieutenant Bunbury took command of the *Eagle* at the end of December 1800, no further actions involving the cutter were recorded. The undeclared war with France was drawing to a close, and the new captain was told by Secretary Stoddert to ''treat public and private armed vessels of France exactly as you find they treat American trading vessels." With the usual post-war economizing—the war had cost the young government more than six million dollars—the second *Eagle* was sold at Baltimore in June 1801, for $10,600.

During the first two decades of United States independence, a diplomatic campaign was waged with England. Its purpose was to wrest from her a fair share of trade with continental Europe. Grievances increased in the early 1800s. American seamen, while ashore in British ports, were impressed into service on British ships. Since England was at war with France, she maintained her right to search neutral American ships and to seize what she considered to be contraband. It was intolerable, however, for Americans to be treated as colonists thirty years after the Revolution; President James Madison declared war on 18 June 1812.

During the first two years of the war, England was too busy with France to spare many ships. However, when Napoleon was exiled to Elba in the spring of 1814, the American coast was blockaded by the full power of the British Navy. Revenue cutters, again cooperating with the United States Navy, did their share to protect the eastern seaboard and permit some coastal commerce.

By the fall of 1814, several British ships had been captured, but two cutters had been lost to the enemy.

The third cutter to carry the name *Eagle* met the enemy bravely, but she too became a victim of the superior British forces. She was a relatively new schooner–rigged cutter, built in 1809 for the Port of New Haven,

Connecticut. She was armed with four 4-pounders and a pair of 2-pounders, and was commanded by Captain Frederick Lee. Lee was a noted Connecticut mariner who served as a state representative, founded Lee's Academy in Madison, Connecticut, and in 1797, while a merchant captain, brought the Polish revolutionary war hero, Thaddeus Kosciusko, back to the United States.

The *Eagle*'s job during the War of 1812 was to convoy American ships through Long Island Sound, since British men-of-war often entered the Sound in pursuit of American merchant vessels.

The sloop *Susan* of New Haven, under Captain Miles, was one of several packets that plied the Sound between New Haven and New York. She was returning to her home port in October, 1814, with a valuable cargo of flour, gunpowder, and dry goods, and with sixteen passengers, when she was captured by a tender from the British frigate *Pomone*.

Upon hearing of the incident, the *Eagle*'s Captain Lee quickly recruited about thirty volunteers in New Haven to reinforce her crew and gave chase. An English 18-gun brig, *Dispatch*, accompanied by her armed tender and a sloop, chased the *Eagle*. Light breezes prevented the cutter from out-maneuvering this far superior assembly of guns, so Captain Lee wisely headed for the Long Island shore and beached the cutter beneath a bluff at Negros Head. The crew dragged two of the 4-pounder guns and both of the 2-pounders up onto the bluff to defend their ship. For six hours a battle raged. When the British were unable to drive the men off the bluff, they tried to destroy the cutter.

The adamant men on the hill withstood repeated attacks, which continued through the night. When the wadding for their guns had been used, the crew tore apart the ship's log. They even picked up the enemy's shot from the ground and fired it back. Through it all, the American flag was kept flying, though on two occasions it required heroic acts to keep it so.

What was left of the cutter the next day was refloated by the New Haven volunteers, but the *Eagle*'s worn crew could not keep her from the superior forces against them. The third *Eagle* was finally taken by the British.

After the war the Treasury Department commissioned William Doughty, a naval architect and constructor, to design three new classes of cutters to replace those lost during the war. Each design was modeled on the Baltimore clipper. The dimensions of the largest class were to be: 79 tons, 69 feet on deck, 19-foot beam, and a 7-foot depth of hold. The fourth and fifth cutters named *Eagle* were constructed from this design. Little is known about these two cutters. Records show that the first was built at New York in 1816 and was intended for duty in Boston, although she was actually assigned to New Haven throughout her career. The second was probably built at Portsmouth, New Hampshire, in 1824 and stationed in New Haven until 1829. Both cutters were commanded by the same Frederick Lee who was skipper of the third *Eagle* during the War of 1812. While commanding the fourth *Eagle* in 1819, Captain

Lee distinguished himself in a daring rescue off Montauk Point, a feat for which he received a handsome silver pitcher engraved with the details of the event.

The careers of these two cutters most likely consisted of the routine duties of revenue cutters: insuring collection of customs duties, capturing contraband, and rescuing life and property endangered by storm or mishaps at sea.

Nearly a century passed before the Coast Guard revived the name *Eagle,* this time for a 100-foot patrol boat. One of thirteen in her class, she was built at Bay City, Michigan by Defoe Boat and Motor Works and was commissioned 11 November 1925. This *Eagle* arrived at her assignment, New London, Connecticut, a month later. During the ensuing seven years there, she was engaged in enforcing an unpopular law: prohibition.

New London was the home of Base Four, one of the busiest operations in the Coast Guard's rum-chasing activities. An estimated one-third of all liquor smuggled into the country in the 1920s came from Rum Row, that notorious anchorage of supply ships just beyond the three-mile limit. The contact boats swarmed to these ships. The ever increasing fleet of Coast Guard craft was kept busy, picketing contact boats and an occasional brazen supply ship until contraband could be seized. Picketing and seizure comprised the duties of the sixth American *Eagle.*

This ship had a 210-ton displacement, a 23-foot beam and an 8-foot draft. She was equipped with two diesel engines, which drove her at 10 knots, not fast enough to catch many of the "rummies." Her armament was a single 3-inch 23-caliber gun, which was sufficient to stop anything in her range.

A typical incident in the *Eagle*'s rum-chasing career occurred in the late 1920s on a dark night, about 40 miles south of Nantucket. *Firelight,* a rum ship or "black," as such ships were called, was already known to the Coast Guard. A year earlier her operators had been taken, convicted, and released by a typically lenient court. The *Eagle* had taken over the trailing of the black from a destroyer, also stationed at Base Four.

The cutter started picketing the *Firelight* at midnight. About twenty minutes later the *Firelight* swerved, opened her engines, and came at the *Eagle,* which was drifting nearby. The cutter quickly reversed engines to avoid the black, but her starboard side was struck lightly. No serious damage was done to the cutter, but the crew of the *Firelight* had misjudged the *Eagle*'s strength. The *Firelight* began to sink, her underwater planking broken. The eight men aboard jumped into the water, where they were picked up by the destroyer and taken to New London to face charges.

In September 1932, the sixth *Eagle* was given a permanent change of station to Charleston, South Carolina. The duties assigned her were similar to those she had been performing in New London. However, the new presidential administration soon ended the "noble experiment" of Prohibition, and the following July other duties were found for the cutter at Charlotte, New York, and on the shores of Lake Ontario. A year later, the ten-year-old ship was sold.

The traditions of service developed by her predecessors are maintained in the seventh cutter bearing the name *Eagle*. Like her predecessors and all Coast Guard cutters, the barque *Eagle* performs multiple missions. She has on numerous occasions been diverted to Search and Rescue missions and medical evacuations. In port she supports the public relations program of the Coast Guard Academy, the Coast Guard, and at times, the nation. During the nation's bicentennial, she acted as host ship for Operation Sail. Her primary mission, however, is to train cadets in seamanship under sail. This mission emphasizes the Coast Guard's firm belief in the value of sail training even in an age of gas turbines.

The training of cadets began in May 1877, aboard the topsail schooner *J. C. Dobbin*. Captain J. A. Henriques had two lieutenants and a few petty officers to assist him in instruction. The curriculum was composed of seamanship and navigation, and the ship sailed for five months between the United States and Bermuda. When she docked at New Bedford, Massachusetts for the winter, academic subjects were added to the curriculum, and the first civilian professor was added to the staff.

The following year the *J. C. Dobbin* was replaced by the *Chase,* a 106-foot barque. New Bedford remained the home port of the *Chase* from 1878 to 1890. After the suspension of "academy training," which lasted from 1890 to 1894, the *Chase* moored for the winter in various southern ports until 1900, when winter quarters were established ashore at Arundel Cove, near Baltimore, Maryland.

Coming ashore did not mean giving up sail training. The *Chase* served until 1907 as the Academy training ship. European cruises, which had started in the 1880s, were continued. When the *Chase* was converted into a barracks ship at Arundel Cove in 1907, she was replaced by a former Naval Academy practice ship, the *Bancroft,* which the Coast Guard renamed *Itasca.*

The next cadet training ship was the *Alexander Hamilton,* the third ship to be named after the founder of the Coast Guard. She had formerly been the naval gunboat, *Vicksburg,* which saw service in China after her launching in 1898, and later was used as one of the state of Washington's Naval Militia practice vessels. She was turned over to the Coast Guard in 1921 and remained in service until 1930. Meanwhile, the Academy had moved from Arundel Cove to New London, locating first at historic Fort Trumbull in 1910 and moving to its present site in 1932. Until 1954, the mainmast from the *Hamilton* served as the Academy's flagpole.

The Academy did not own a large training ship from 1930 until 1946, when it acquired the *Horst Wessel.* Still, sail training was carried out on a fleet of smaller craft: a two-masted Gloucester fishing schooner, the *J. C. Dobbin II,* renamed *Chase;* a 65-foot schooner yacht, *Curlew;* the famous three-masted, 185-foot ocean racing schooner, *Atlantic,* and a number of minor yachts and dinghies. In these, cadets learned the rudiments of seamanship.

A most fortunate aid to Academy sail training occurred when the Danish full-rigged training ship, *Danmark,* was placed by her captain, Knud L. Hansen, at the disposal of the United States. This came as a result of Hitler's invasion of Denmark. From January 1942 to September 1945, officers and crew taught cadets to handle the 700-ton ship in every sea condition. The *Danmark*'s mainmast still bears a bronze plaque commemorating her wartime service in the U.S. Coast Guard.

When World War II ended, the Danes said fond goodbyes, and the Academy looked for another training ship. Such a ship was found in Germany.

After the war, there were three German barques to be shared by the Allied victors as war reparations: The *Gorch Foch* went to the Soviet Union, and was renamed *Tovarisch;* the *Albert Leo Schlageter* went to Brazil but was later sold to Portugal and became *Sagres II;* and the *Horst Wessel* went to the United States and became the seventh *Eagle*.

This 1816-ton, 295-foot barque was built in Hamburg in 1936 by Blohm and Voss. Named *Horst Wessel,* after an early lieutenant of Hitler, she served the German Navy for ten years as a training ship, making cruises to the Canary Islands and West Indies. During World War II, she operated in the Baltic Sea, sometimes transporting supplies to and refugees from East Prussia. Her log records that she fired at Allied planes at least once, and that Hitler's birthday was dutifully observed on board.

In January 1946, Commander Gordan McGowan, who had been teaching seamanship to cadets, was ordered to head a group of ten officers and Coast Guardsmen as the nucleus of a crew to bring the present *Eagle* to the Academy from Bremerhaven, Germany.

Refitting the ship for sea in wartorn Germany took five months, after which German sailors were recruited to supplement the Coast Guard crew. The return trip was made in June and July, by the triangular Madeira-Bermuda-New York route, along which the inexperienced crew ran into a hurricane. But the seventh *Eagle* dispelled any doubts the skipper might have had about her seaworthiness. Although he brought his ship into New York Harbor with unseamanlike shreds of sail draped over her spars, his ship and crew arrived safely.

When the Coast Guard took over this *Eagle* at Bremerhaven, the figurehead was coincidentally a handsome carved eagle. Its talons held a wreath, inside which was a swastika, the symbol of the Nazis. The eagle remained, but the swastika was replaced by the shield of the United States Coast Guard. The original figurehead deteriorated and has been replaced several times. The current figurehead was fabricated in 1976 of mahogany, with a stainless steel rod, ensuring a longevity equal to that of barque *Eagle*.

Each year since 1948 the *Eagle* has been an integral part of the Academy's summer professional training program. Accompanied by modern cutters, or alone, she has cruised the entire North Atlantic and visited almost every major port on both sides. On occasion she has passed through the Panama Canal and cruised on the West Coast. Whenever her schedule has permitted, she has participated in the British Sail

Training Association Races, competing against other "Tall Ships" from Europe, South America, and even Asia. Perhaps the symbolic high point of her career occurred on the Fourth of July in 1976 when she, as host vessel, led the parade of tall ships into New York Harbor in Operation Sail '76 to celebrate the nation's bicentennial.

The *Eagle* was not designed, nor is she used, as a pleasure ship or a showpiece. Despite her modern equipment, manpower is used for most jobs aboard. The courage and agility a cadet shows in the rigging, the alertness he displays in drills, and his accuracy with navigational instruments are important indications of his future qualities as an officer. Adaptability is the key word in summer training aboard the *Eagle*.

Captain Carl Bowman, as salty a skipper as ever paced a ship's quarterdeck, was once asked by author Alan Villiers, himself a veteran sail-training master, why the Coast Guard retains an anachronism like the *Eagle*. The captain replied, "We can see our boys here all the time, and we get a pretty good idea what they're made of before the voyage is over."

Some 170 cadets can be trained at a time in the *Eagle*, about four times as many as in a more modern cutter. There are economic advantages, of course, but the main reason for sail training is the intimate knowledge of sea and wind that a cadet acquires in the *Eagle*. In addition, upper classmen on board gain experience in leadership essential to their performance as officers.

This philosophy of sail training is reflected in the U.S. Coast Guard Academy mission:

To graduate young men and women with sound bodies, stout hearts, and alert minds, with a liking for the sea and its lore, and with a high sense of honor, loyalty, and obedience which goes with trained initiative and leadership; well-grounded in seamanship, the sciences, and the amenities; and strong in the resolve to be worthy of the traditions of the commissioned officers in the United States Coast Guard in the service of their country and humanity.

That is the mission, too, of this seventh *Eagle*, a name engraved deeply in the traditions of the Coast Guard, traditions nearly as old as the nation.

2. Compartmentation and Standing Rigging

The language of the sea is ancient. To the polliwog, it is complex but eminently practical. Every fitting on the ship and every action performed by its crew has its proper designation. By using the correct terminology, commands can be given quickly, efficiently, and safely. Thus, it is important for cadets to learn the correct nautical terms for describing the various parts of the ship and its evolutions. In the following chapters, important nautical terms have been italicized. The Glossary contains definitions of those terms not defined in the text.

HULL CONSTRUCTION

The *Eagle* is built of German steel on the transverse framing system. The details of construction are very similar to American practices of the same period. When this vessel was built, the technique of full welding had not yet been developed. In general, the seams are riveted and the butts are welded. Fittings are generally bolted on while strength members, such as knees and gussets, are welded to the frames. The plating is approximately $4/10$-inch thick.

There are two full length steel decks, a platform deck below these, and a raised forecastle and quarter-deck. The weatherdecks have a 3-inch teak deck laid on top of the steel. The second deck has a 3-inch pine deck covered with vinyl tile. The platform deck and the tank tops are steel.

The second deck is the damage control deck. There are six watertight bulkheads which run to the main deck but which have watertight doors on the second (or living) deck level.

Figures 1 and 2 show the various compartments on the *Eagle*. The compartments are designated, in accordance with standard Navy practice, by three numbers and a letter. The first number indicates the deck on which the compartment is located. 1 is the main deck, 2, the second deck and so forth. Decks above the main deck begin with Ø; thus, on the *Eagle* the bridge is the Ø1 deck, the top of the deck house the Ø2 deck, etc. The second number of the compartment number indicates the frame nearest the forward end of the compartment. The final number indicates whether the compartment is port or starboard. Compartments to starboard have odd numbers, those to port have even numbers. Compartments that extend the entire width

Figure 1. Damage Control Diagram.

Length (counter to tip of bowsprit)	295 ft.
(counter to tip of bowsprit)	277 ft.
(without bowsprit)	
(at water line)	231 ft.
Greatest beam	39.1 ft.
Freeboard	9.1 ft.
Draft (fully loaded)	17 ft.
Displacement (fully loaded)	1,816 tons
Volume (gross tonnage)	1,500 B.R.T.
Ballast (iron pigs)	344 tons
Fuel oil	24,215 gal.
Foretruck (height above water line)	147.3 ft.
Maintruck	147.3 ft.
Mizzentruck	132 ft.
Fore and Mainyard	78.8 ft.
Sail area	21,350 sq. ft.
Auxiliary motor (M.A.N. Diesel)	728 h.p.
Speed under power (flat calm)	9.3 knots
Anchors (two patent)	
starboard	3,800 lbs.
port	3,500 lbs.
Chain (diameter 1.75 inches)	135 fathoms/
	9 shots on each chain

superstructure deck

KEY

Dotted lines and cross-hatching indicates boundaries and fittings hidden from view. Dot-dash line indicates intersection of horizontal level with vertical bulkhead.

Quick acting watertight (W.T.) or airtight (A.T.) door. Weight of bulkhead line indicates type of door.

Watertight (W.T.) or airtight (A.T.) door. Weight of bulkhead indicates type of door.

Fumetight (F.T.) flametight (M.T.) or non-tight (N.T.) door.

Arch or opening.

Hatch.

Hatchway.

Hatch, operable from above or below.

Manhole.

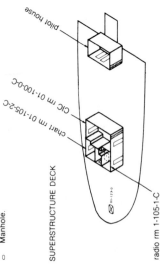

SUPERSTRUCTURE DECK

pilot house

chart rm 01-105-2-C

CIC rm 01-100-0-C

radio rm 1-105-1-C

MAIN DECK

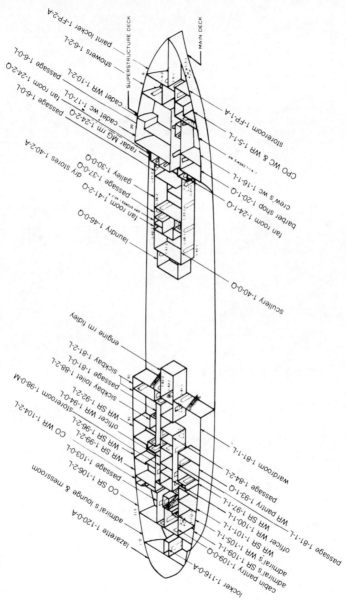

paint locker 1-FP-2-A
showers 1-6-2-L
cadet WR 1-10-2-L
passage 1-6-0-L
fan room 1-24-2-O
passage 1-6-0-L
cadet WR 1-17-0-L
radar MG rm 1-24-2-O
dry stores 1-40-2-A
passage 1-37-0-O
galley 1-30-0-O
fan room 1-41-2-O
laundry 1-46-0-O
scullery 1-40-0-O

SUPERSTRUCTURE DECK
MAIN DECK

storeroom 1-FP-1-A
WR 1-5-1-L
CPO WC & WR 1-8-1-L
crew s wc 1-16-1-L
barber shop 1-20-1-O
fan room 1-24-1-O

engine rm l'dley

passage 1-81-2-L
sickbay 1-81-2-L
passage 1-81-0-L
sickbay toilet 1-88-2-L
officer WR 1-94-0-L
WR SR 1-92-2-L
storeroom 1-98-0-M
WR SR 1-96-2-L
WR SR 1-99-2-L
passage 1-103-0-L
CO SR 1-106-2-L
admiral's lounge & messroom
lazarette 1-120-0-A
locker 1-116-0-A
cabin pantry 1-109-0-O
admiral's SR 1-105-1-L

CO WR 1-104-2-L

wardroom 1-81-1-L
passage 1-84-2-L
WR pantry 1-93-1-O
WR SR 1-97-1-L
officer WR 1-100-1-L
WR SR 1-101-1-L
admiral's WR 1-105-1-L

SECOND DECK

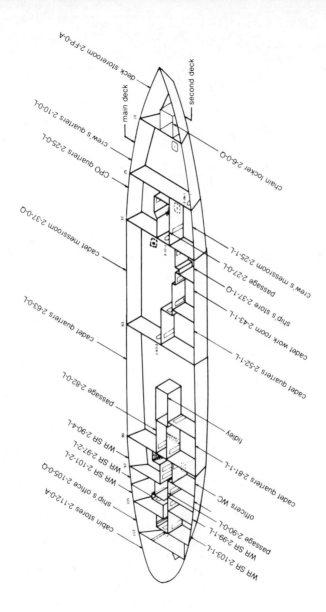

deck storeroom 2-FP-0-A

main deck

second deck

crew's quarters 2-10-0-L

CPO quarters 2-25-0-L

chain locker 2-6-0-O

cadet messroom 2-37-0-O

cadet's messroom 2-25-1-L

passage 2-27-0-L

ship's store 2-37-1-O

cadet quarters 2-63-0-L

cadet work room 2-43-1-L

cadet quarters 2-52-1-L

passage 2-82-0-L

WR SR 2-90-4-L

WR SR 2-97-2-L

WR SR 2-101-2-L

ship's office 2-105-0-O

cabin stores 2-112-0-A

WR SR 2-103-1-L

passage 2-90-0-L

officers WC

cadet quarters 2-81-1-L

tidley

FIRST PLATFORM

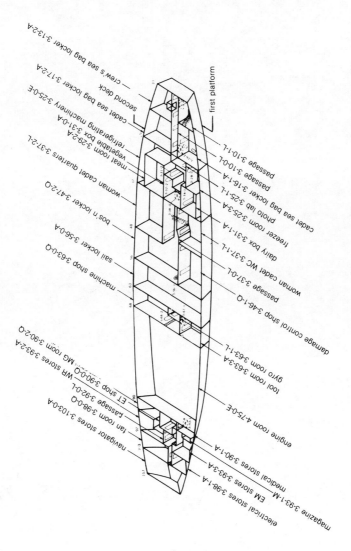

crew's sea bag locker 3-13-2-A
cadet sea bag locker 3-17-2-A
second deck
refrigerating machinery 3-25-0-E
vegetable box 3-31-0-A
meal room 3-29-2-A
woman cadet quarters 3-37-2-L
bos'n locker 3-47-2-O
sail locker 3-56-0-A
machine shop 3-63-0-O

first platform
passage 3-10-1-L
passage 3-10-0-L
cadet sea bag locker 3-25-1-L
photo lab 3-25-3-A
freezer room 3-25-3-A
dairy box 3-37-1-L
woman cadet WC 3-37-0-L
passage 3-37-0-L
damage control shop 3-46-1-O

navigator stores 3-103-0-A
electrical stores 3-98-1-A
WR stores 3-93-2-A
ET shop 3-92-0-L
passage 3-92-0-L
fan room 3-98-0-O
MG room 3-90-2-O
passage 3-90-0-O

magazine 3-93-1-M
EM stores 3-93-3-A
medical stores 3-90-1-A
engine room 4-75-0-E
gyro room 3-63-3-A
tool room 3-63-3-A
damage control shop 3-46-1-O

Figure 2. Damage Control Diagram.

HOLD

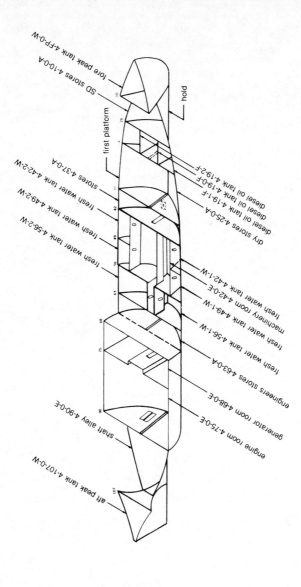

fore peak tank 4-FP-0-W
SD stores 4-10-0-A
hold
first platform
diesel oil tank 4-19-2-F
diesel oil tank 4-19-0-F
diesel oil tank 4-19-1-F
dry stores 4-25-0-A
fresh water tank 4-42-2-W
stores 4-37-0-A
fresh water tank 4-49-2-W
fresh water tank 4-56-2-W
fresh water tank 4-42-1-W
machinery room 4-42-0-E
fresh water tank 4-49-1-W
fresh water tank 4-56-1-W
engineers stores 4-63-0-A
generator room 4-68-0-E
engine room 4-75-0-E
shaft alley 4-90-0-E
aft peak tank 4-107-0-W

of the ship are listed as Ø. The letter that follows the three numbers indicates the use of the compartment. For example, L is used for living spaces, E for machinery spaces, and F for fuel tanks. The compartment number of the main cadet berthing area is 2-63-Ø-L. This indicates that it is on the second deck, its forward bulkhead is at frame 63, it extends the entire width of the ship, and it is used as a living space.

The main deck of the *Eagle* contains the heads and showers for the male cadets and crew. These are located under the forecastle. Also in this area is the forward damage control locker (Repair II). Aft of this are the galley, scullery, and laundry. The aft section of the main deck, beneath the quarterdeck, contains officers' quarters and consists of the cabin, the wardroom, and the officers' staterooms. The sick bay is located on the port side of the main deck, opposite the wardroom. The second deck is the main living deck. The crew's quarters are forward, followed by the crew's lounge and the chief petty officers' mess. The next space aft on the port side is the mess deck, which is also used for classroom training. The ship's store and berthing spaces are located on the starboard side. The main cadet berthing area is in the next compartment aft. The aft damage control locker (Repair III) is located in this berthing area. The lower wardroom area and the ship's office are located all the way aft.

The third deck contains the various workshops and storerooms needed to operate the ship. Forward are the sea-bag lockers, followed by the reefer flat. Amidships under the mess-deck are the sail-locker, boatswain's hold, damage control shop and the female cadet berthing area and head. Under the main cadet berthing area are the machine and electrical shops and the gyrocompass room. The lowest deck in the *Eagle* is devoted completely to the various fuel and water tanks, storage areas, and machinery spaces.

While the number of compartments may be confusing, their location and use must be quickly learned. In an emergency, all hands may be called to assist damage control parties in any part of the ship.

MASTS AND SPARS

The lower masts, topmasts, topgallant masts, royal masts, bowsprit, yards, booms, and mizzen gaff on the *Eagle* are all made of hollow steel tubes. All of these are known as spars. The foremast is *stepped* on the second deck, the mainmast is stepped on the keel, and the mizzenmast is stepped on the platform deck over the *shaft alley*. The fore and main masts, and their yards, are identical. As shown in figures 3 and 4 the *Eagle* follows the rigging practices of large sailing ships in their final stage of development. The foremast and its topmast are really one hollow tube, as are the mainmast and its topmast. However, they are rigged as the older vessels were: the shrouds (wire rope cables which support the masts) come in under the tops, where a new system of topmast shrouds originates. The two parts of the masts retain their original names: foremast from the deck to the top and foretopmast from the top to the cross-trees. The same applies to the main. The topgallant and royal masts are each a hollow

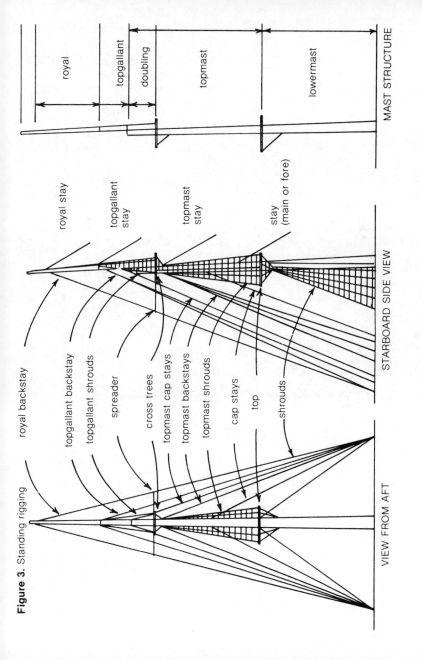

Figure 3. Standing rigging

royal

topgallant

doubling

topmast

lowermast

MAST STRUCTURE

royal stay

topgallant stay

topmast stay

stay (main or fore)

STARBOARD SIDE VIEW

royal backstay

topgallant backstay

topgallant shrouds

spreader

cross trees

topmast cap stays

topmast backstays

topmast shrouds

cap stays

top

shrouds

VIEW FROM AFT

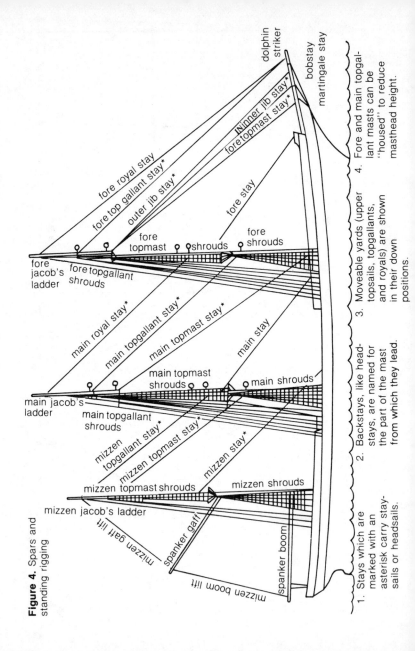

Figure 4. Spars and standing rigging

1. Stays which are marked with an asterisk carry staysails or headsails.

2. Backstays, like headstays, are named for the part of the mast from which they lead.

3. Moveable yards (upper topsails, topgallants, and royals) are shown in their down positions.

4. Fore and main topgallant masts can be "housed" to reduce masthead height.

dolphin striker

bobstay

martingale stay

inner jib stay*

fore topmast stay*

fore royal stay

fore top gallant stay*

outer jib stay*

fore stay

fore topmast

fore shrouds

shrouds

fore jacob's ladder

fore topgallant shrouds

main royal stay*

main topgallant stay*

main topmast stay*

main stay

main topmast shrouds

main shrouds

main jacob's ladder

main topgallant shrouds

mizzen topgallant stay*

mizzen topmast stay*

mizzen stay*

mizzen topmast shrouds

mizzen shrouds

mizzen jacob's ladder

mizzen gaff lift

spanker gaff

spanker boom

mizzen boom lift

steel spar, but the topgallant shrouds terminate about halfway up the spar. The portion above the topgallant *hounds* is known as the royal mast. The following table gives the names and weights of the individual spars:

Name of spar	Length	Weight
Bowsprit	43 feet	7300 lbs.
Topgallant Masts	49 feet	2128 lbs.
Fore and Main Yards	79 feet	6380 lbs.
Lower Topsail Yards	72 feet	4840 lbs.
Upper Topsail Yards	63 feet	3520 lbs.
Topgallant Yards	50 feet	1700 lbs.
Royal Yards	38 feet	884 lbs.
Mizzen Gaff	35 feet	994 lbs.
Mizzen Boom	54 feet	2200 lbs.

STANDING RIGGING

In a sailing vessel there are two types of rigging: standing rigging, which supports the masts, and running rigging, which is used to *set, douse,* and *trim* the sails.

Since the standing rigging must support the masts against the tremendous strain of the wind on the sails, it is made of high-strength wire rope. This rigging is not adjustable, and much of it is *wormed, parceled,* and *served* to protect it from corrosion.

The three most important types of standing rigging are the stays, the shrouds, and the backstays:

1. *Stays* provide fore-and-aft support for the masts. They provide almost all of the support for the masts when the sails are *caught aback* (with wind blowing on the front rather than on the back side). Since there are only a few stays for each mast, it

is dangerous to be caught aback in high winds.

The *bobstay* on the *Eagle* is a steel rod which runs from the bow, just above the water line, to the *bowsprit* giving it support and allowing it to take the strain of the stays which lead to the foremast.

As illustrated in figure 4, the stays are named for the part of the mast *to which* they lead. The headsails and staysails are *bent* to these stays, the staysails being named for the stay to which they are bent.

2. *Shrouds* provide athwartship support for the masts. On the *Eagle* there are three sets of shrouds, two of which are on the mizzen. The lower set leads from the deck to the *tops* (lower platforms named for the "Fighting Tops" where marines were stationed in battle). The middle set (topmast shrouds) leads from the top to just below the *cross-trees* (the upper platform). The upper set (royal shrouds) leads from the cross-trees to just below the truck (top of the mast).

Futtock (from Foot-hook) *shrouds* are steel rods leading from the futtock band below the tops to the edge of the tops. They provide a foundation for the topmast shrouds.

Ratlines are tarred hemp lines *seized* to the shrouds to form a "ladder" by which cadets may lay aloft. *Crane lines* are wire ropes which lead from the shrouds athwartship to the masts. They provide a footing for cadets furling and unfurling the staysails.

3. *Backstays* provide diagonal support to the aft side of the masts and bear the bulk of the strain of the wind against the sails.

Other pieces of standing rigging include *footropes*, which are wire ropes hung from *stirrups* under the yards to provide footing; *flemish horses*, which are loops of wire rope providing footing at the ends of the yards; and *lifts* (except for the course lift, which is adjustable), which support the upper three yards when the sails are not set.

3. Sails and Running Rigging

The *Eagle*'s twenty-two sails drive her, in optimum winds, twice as fast as does her auxiliary engine. The sails are set, doused, and trimmed by means of her running rigging. The task of memorizing the location and use of the more than 170 lines may at first seem overwhelming, but it is actually quite simple. The lines can be grouped into a handful of functions; their locations are logically determined by their functions. In addition, most lines are paired and located similarly on the fore and main masts. To understand these functions it will first be necessary to examine the *Eagle*'s sails (see figure 5).

SQUARE SAILS

The *Eagle* has ten square sails. The sails on the foremast and mainmast are essentially the same and are made of panels of dacron. The *head* of the sail is attached to the forward *jackstay* on the *yard* by *robands*. *Earrings* in the upper corners of the sails are attached to a hook on the earring jackstay and keep the head of the sail taut. The side edges of the sail are the *leeches;* the bottom edge is the *foot;* and the lower

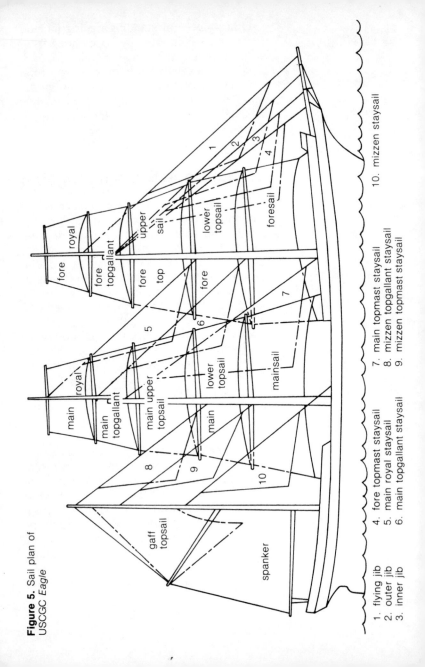

Figure 5. Sail plan of USCGC *Eagle*

fore royal

fore topgallant

fore upper topsail

fore top

fore lower topsail

foresail

main royal

main topgallant

main upper topsail

main lower topsail

mainsail

gaff topsail

spanker

1. flying jib
2. outer jib
3. inner jib
4. fore topmast staysail
5. main royal staysail
6. main topgallant staysail
7. main topmast staysail
8. mizzen topgallant staysail
9. mizzen topmast staysail
10. mizzen staysail

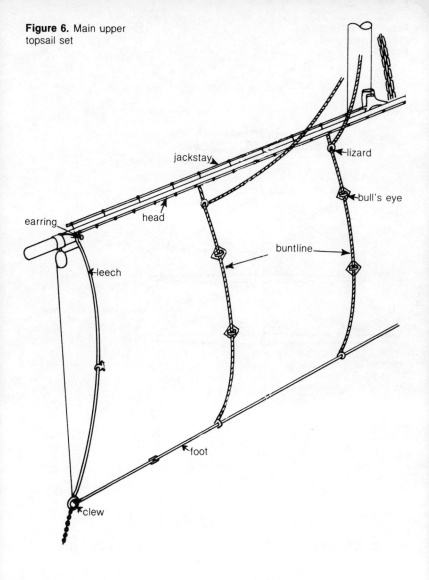

Figure 6. Main upper topsail set

jackstay

lizard

head

bull's eye

earring

buntline

leech

foot

clew

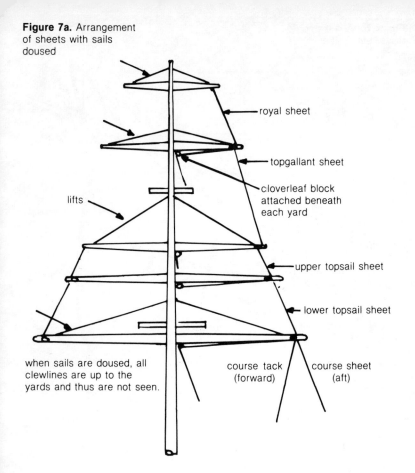

Figure 7a. Arrangement of sheets with sails doused

royal sheet

topgallant sheet

cloverleaf block attached beneath each yard

lifts

upper topsail sheet

lower topsail sheet

when sails are doused, all clewlines are up to the yards and thus are not seen.

course tack (forward)

course sheet (aft)

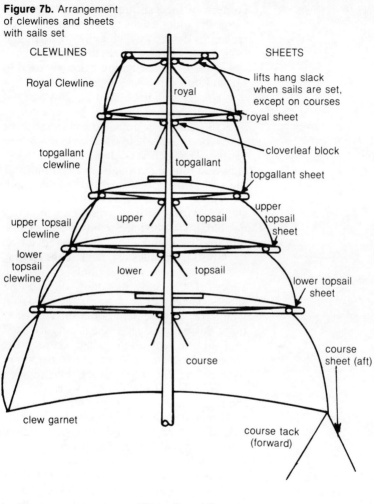

Figure 7b. Arrangement of clewlines and sheets with sails set

CLEWLINES

SHEETS

Royal Clewline

royal

lifts hang slack
when sails are set,
except on courses

royal sheet

topgallant
clewline

topgallant

cloverleaf block

topgallant sheet

upper topsail
clewline

upper topsail

upper
topsail
sheet

lower
topsail
clewline

lower topsail

lower topsail
sheet

course

course
sheet (aft)

clew garnet

course tack
(forward)

all clewlines except for
the course, are handled
from the pinrails

the portion of the
sheet that renders
through the cheek
blocks is made
of chain

all sheets, except for the
course, are handled from
the fiferails

corners of the sail are the *clews*. Running along the outer edges of the sails is a wide *tabling* of dacron, which helps to shape the sails and give them strength (figure 6).

The bulk of the running rigging is used to set and douse the sails (see figures 6–8):

1. *Sheets* are attached to the clews of the sails and are used to sheet the sails home, i.e., to haul them down to the next lower yard—or the deck for the *courses*—when setting. The section of sheet attached to the clew and running through the sheet block at the end of the lower yard is made of chain to reduce chafing; the remainder of the sheet is wire rope with a single sheave runner block attached at the bitter end. A manila line dead-ended on deck is reeved on deck through a block and back to the *fiferail*.

2. *Clewlines* are also attached to the clews of the sails but they oppose the sheets. Clewlines lead up to the yards on which the sails are bent rather than down to the yards below. Just as the sheets are used to haul the sail down when setting, the clewlines (*clew garnets* on the courses) are used to haul the sail up when dousing.

3. *Buntlines* are also used when dousing the sail. If just the clewlines were used, the sails would belly out in the wind so much that they could not be furled. In heavy winds, they would probably *luff* violently. The buntlines run from the foot of the sails through *bull's-eyes* in the sails, which allow the line to gather the sail up to the yard in several small bights. The *lizards* at the head of the sails are *fair-leads* for the buntlines.

4. *Leechlines* are used on the courses because their leeches are so long that they are difficult to handle when dousing. The lines

lead from the middle of the leeches up to the yard. On the topgallant and royals, the leechlines and outer-buntlines are combined into *bunt-leechlines*, which lead from the yard to the leech and then to the posi-

Figure 8. the mainsail.

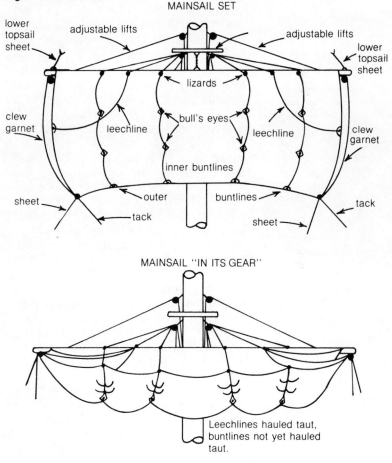

MAINSAIL SET

lower topsail sheet

adjustable lifts

adjustable lifts

lower topsail sheet

lizards

clew garnet

leechline

bull's eyes

leechline

clew garnet

inner buntlines

sheet

outer

buntlines

tack

tack

sheet

MAINSAIL "IN ITS GEAR"

Leechlines hauled taut, buntlines not yet hauled taut.

tion on the foot of the sail where a buntline would normally be attached. The two functions are combined since the foot of these sails is short enough that it can be handled by a single buntline in combination with the bunt-leechline. The topsails do not have leechlines because their leeches are so short that they are easily handled when dousing.

5. *Tacks* are used only on the courses. Unlike the upper sails, the courses are not set onto a lower yard. Thus, it is impossible to control the foot of the sail by a single line, for when braced sharp, the lead of the weather sheet is excessively long. Tacks, then, serve the same function as sheets but lead forward whereas the sheets lead aft. In setting the courses, the tacks and sheets are balanced so as to hold the foot of the sail directly under the course yard. When braced sharp, the weather edge of the sail is often flattened by means of a *tack jigger,* a three-fold purchase attached to a pendant on the clew and to a padeye on deck.

6. *Halyards* (from haul yard) are used in raising the upper three yards in setting sail. The upper three sails are set by hauling the sail down to the lower yard and then hauling the yard up until the sail sets properly. The yards are moveable for two reasons. Having the yard down when the sail is not set lowers the center of gravity and thus improves the ship's ride in a seaway. More importantly, it is much easier to set and douse the sails with a moveable yard: when the sails are sheeted home they will still spill most of the wind and allow the sheets to be hauled down with relative ease. Then the sail can be fully set by hauling on a

single line with a large mechanical advantage—the halyard—instead of the two sheets whose mechanical advantage is much smaller. The lower two yards are fixed and therefore do not have halyards.

The six types of line discussed above account for almost half of all the running rigging. As will be seen later in the chapter, their location on the pinrails and fiferails is logically determined by their function. As a result, learning the lines for the square sails should not present any major difficulties.

HEADSAILS AND STAYSAILS

The *Eagle* has six staysails, named after the part of the mast supported by the stay on which they are bent, and four headsails. Like the square sails, all are made of dacron. The leading edge of the sail is the *luff*. Metal *hanks* are used to bend the luff to its stay. The bottom edge is the *foot,* as in a square sail, while the aft edge is the *leech*. The top point of the sail, to which the halyard is bent, is the *head;* the lower point, at the junction of the foot and the luff, to which the tack pendant is attached, is the *tack;* and the remaining point at the junction of the foot and the leech, to which the sheet is attached, is the *clew*. Along the edge of the sail, as with square sails, is a tabling of dacron. *Eagle*'s headsails and staysails are Scotch-cut. The panels of dacron parallel the leech or the foot and are joined at the miter seam which runs from the clew to the luff (see figure 9).

Three lines control the headsails and staysails. A fourth, the tack pendant, runs from the tack to the mast on the staysails and to the bowsprit on the headsails. It is used to hold the sail at the proper distance up the stay. This pendant is permanently attached and is not adjustable.

1. *Halyards* are bent to the heads of the sails and are used for setting them by hauling the luffs up the stay.

2. *Sheets,* as on square sails, are attached to the sails and are used for trimming them. The headsails have two sheets each, one for each side, and thus can be shifted without dousing. In contrast, the staysails have but a single sheet which must be shifted from side to side. It is impractical to rig dual sheets for the staysails since they are set higher above the deck than the headsails;

Figure 9. Staysail nomenclature.

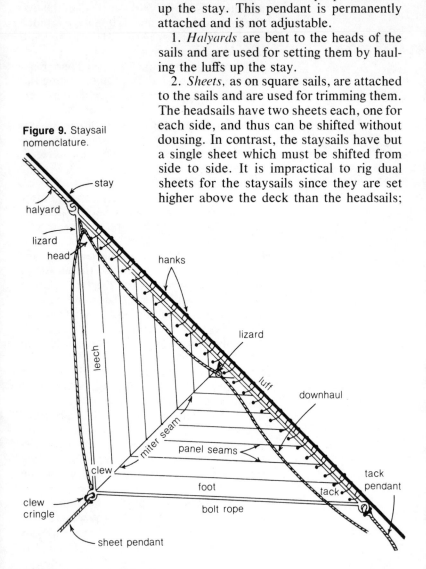

therefore, it would be difficult to pull the sheet over the lower stays from the deck. Moreover, the extra lines rigged in a working area would cause safety problems as they slatted about.

The sheets themselves consist of two parts. A wire-rope sheet pendant is permanently shackled to the clew of the sail. A sheet tackle, whose size depends on the size of the sail, is shackled to an eye on deck and to the pendant. In shifting the sheets, the two shackles are unshackled, and the tackle is carried to the opposite rail. The pendant is hauled up and over any lower stays by a cadet stationed in the top. It is then reshackled into the tackle.

3. *Downhauls*, as the name implies, are used for dousing the sails. They lead to the head of the sails through a lizard at the head and then down to the clew. This arrangement allows better control of the sail in dousing. Hauling on the downhaul will pull the clew of the sail up to the head, causing it to spill its wind and lessen its slatting, and will pull the sail bodily down the stay.

SPANKER AND GAFF TOPSAIL

The two remaining sails, the spanker and gaff topsail, although unique, are rigged in a manner analogous to the squaresails. The spanker's parts bear the same names as those of the square sail, while the gaff topsail's parts bear the same names as those of the stay sail. The upper aft corner of the spanker is known as the *peak*, the upper forward corner as the *throat*, and the lower forward corner at the foot as the *tack* (figure 10). The running rigging for the spanker consists of the following:

1. The *topping lift* is used to top (lift) the spanker boom high enough for the sail to set properly. When the sail is not set, the boom is lowered into a gallows and snugged down to keep it from slatting about.

2. *Outhauls* are analogous to the sheets of the square sails and are used to haul the sail out to the end of the boom (foot outhaul) and gaff (peak outhaul).

3. *Inhauls* are analogous to the clewlines of the square sails and are opposed to the outhauls. They are used to haul the head and foot of the sail back to the mast when dousing.

4. The *brails* are analogous to the buntlines on the square sails and are used to control the body of the spanker when dousing. Since the spanker can be set on either tack, the brails are rigged on both sides of the sail.

5. The *sheet* is a three-fold purchase that runs from an eye on the fantail to the end of the boom. It is used to trim the spanker.

6. The *preventer* is a three-fold purchase used to oppose the sheet. As the sheet leads from midship on the fantail, it cannot control the swing of the boom if the ship gets caught aback and the boom starts to swing to weather. The tremendous momentum developed by more than a ton of gear swinging out of control could easily tear the sail or even rip the boom from the mast. The preventer keeps the boom from swinging and thus prevents uncontrolled *jibes*. One block of the preventer tackle is rigged to the fitting located about one-third of the distance from the end of the boom. The other block is hooked to a padeye on deck at the aft end of the pinrail. If the boom is swung

Figure 10. Spanker.

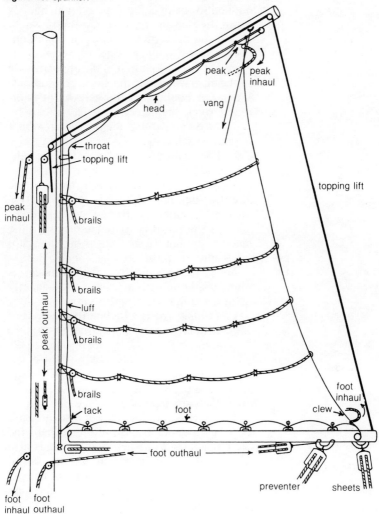

peak

peak inhaul

head

vang

throat

topping lift

peak inhaul

topping lift

brails

peak outhaul

brails

brails

luff

brails

foot inhaul

clew

tack

foot

foot outhaul

preventer

sheets

foot inhaul

foot outhaul

out to its maximum limit, the block is hooked to the eye of a pendant which leads to a fitting on the aft boat davit and which allows the preventer to lead more horizontally. Since only a single preventer is rigged, it must be shifted to the opposite side of the ship whenever the ship comes about. When the boom is in the gallows, it is directly over the sheet padeye. It can be snugged down without the preventer, which is then struck down.

7. The *vangs* are used to control the gaff. In general, they are used only when the sail is not set and prevent the gaff from slatting about. When the spanker is set, the movement of the gaff is controlled by the spanker sheet, to which it is connected through the leech of the sail. In such cases the vangs are used only for trimming.

The gaff topsail, like the spanker, is unique although the lines function exactly as in the other sails (figure 11).

1. The *halyard* is attached to the head of the sail and is used for setting (as with a staysail).

2. The *sheet* is attached to the clew of the sail and is used to haul the leech of the sail to the end of the gaff in setting (as does the sheet of a square sail).

3. The *clewline*, like that of a square sail, opposes the sheet and is used to haul the clew of the sail in when dousing. It is also analogous to the downhaul of a staysail: it leads through a lizard at the head of the sail and thus is also used to haul the sail bodily down the jackstay.

4. The *tacks* are attached to the tack of the sail and are used to adjust the set of the luff and foot of the sail. Two tacks are

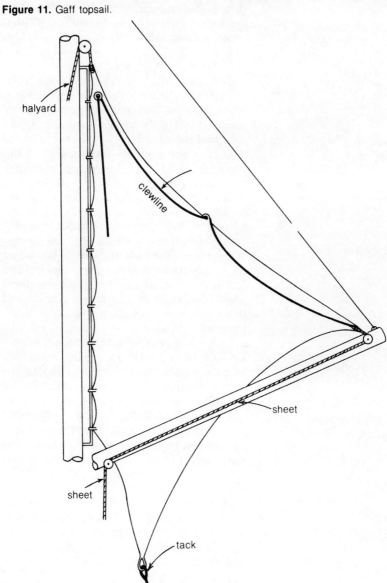

Figure 11. Gaff topsail.

rigged, one on either side of the gaff, so that the tack of the sail can be shifted without sending a man aloft.

LIFTS AND BRACES

The lines discussed so far are used primarily for setting and dousing the sails. The remaining two types of running rigging are used primarily for trimming the square sails and their yards.

1. *Lifts* are used to give support to the yards (figure 12). The upper three yards are moveable and are hauled up to set the sails. When the sails are not set, the yards are settled *into their lifts*. These lifts, which are not adjustable, support the yards and prevent them from working up and down. When the sails are set, the yard is hauled up the mast and the lifts hang slack. The leeches of the sails tie the yards together, preventing the yards from working up and down and allowing all of the yards to be trimmed at once.

The lower topsail yard does not have a lift since it is a fixed yard whose position, when sails are doused, is so close to the upper top yard that it can be controlled by use of the upper topsail sheets.

The main and fore yards have adjustable lifts. A lift pendant leads from the yardarms to the mast and then to deck via a three-fold purchase. The lifts are adjustable so that *cockbill* may be removed and the yards can be trimmed parallel to the horizon, the optimum position for sailing. As mentioned above, all of the yards are tied together, when set, by the leeches of the sails. Thus, by adjusting the course lifts, all five yards will be trimmed simultaneously. The actual

Figure 12. Lifts and braces.

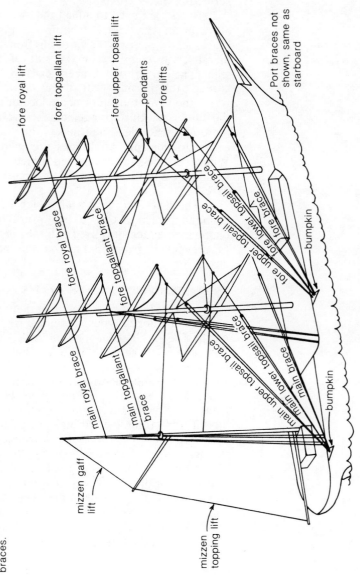

process of removing cockbill will be described in the next chapter.

2. *Braces* are used to adjust the fore and aft trim of the yards. The lower three braces lead directly to the yardarms from the pinrails, via *bumpkins* on the side of the ship. The upper two braces lead up the shrouds (of the mast) aft of the mast, on which the yards they control are located, to the yardarms. This arrangement results in a more horizontal lead and makes the yards easier to control. All braces are paired. Whenever one brace is hauled, its equivalent on the opposite side of the ship must be eased.

3. The *timenoguy* is a whip which leads from the mizzen shrouds to the lower block on the main brace. It is used to lift the brace to prevent it from fouling on the boat davits.

THE LOCATION OF LINES ON THE PINRAILS

By now it should be evident that there are more than a dozen types of running rigging on the *Eagle*. Their location on deck is arranged logically so that it is easy to find any line once the location of a few key lines, which are readily identified, are learned. It is absolutely essential that personnel working the ship memorize the lines since throwing off the wrong line can damage gear or seriously injure personnel. For example, if the halyard for the upper topsail is thrown off by mistake, there is a good possibility that the topgallant sail, which would have to bear the entire weight of the upper topsail yard and its gear, will tear. The tremendous weight of the yard as it slides down its track can part the lifts and result in the yard

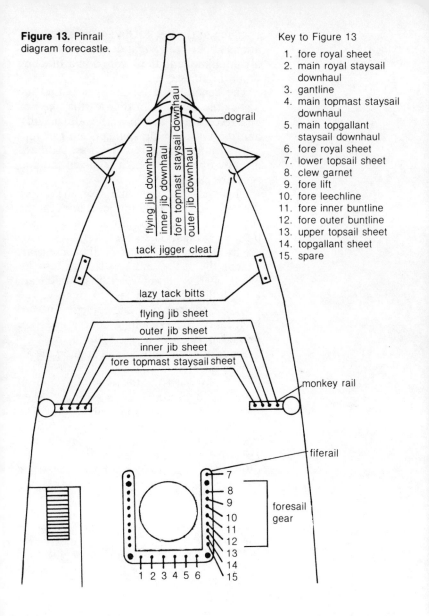

Figure 13. Pinrail diagram forecastle.

Key to Figure 13

1. fore royal sheet
2. main royal staysail downhaul
3. gantline
4. main topmast staysail downhaul
5. main topgallant staysail downhaul
6. fore royal sheet
7. lower topsail sheet
8. clew garnet
9. fore lift
10. fore leechline
11. fore inner buntline
12. fore outer buntline
13. upper topsail sheet
14. topgallant sheet
15. spare

dograil

flying jib downhaul
inner jib downhaul
fore topmast staysail downhaul
outer jib downhaul

tack jigger cleat

lazy tack bitts

flying jib sheet
outer jib sheet
inner jib sheet
fore topmast staysail sheet

monkey rail

fiferail

foresail gear

crashing to the deck. Obviously, safe operations aboard the *Eagle* depend on each individual knowing the location and function of all the lines.

The general rule for all lines is that the higher the sail, the further aft the line will be. Except for the halyards, downhauls, and the lines for the spanker and gaff topsail, all lines are paired and are positioned directly opposite to each other on the pinrails and fiferails.

Clewlines and buntlines for the upper four square sails and bunt-leechlines for the royals and topgallants are grouped by sail on the pinrails. The sheets for these sails are located on the fiferails. All course gear, except the tacks and sheets, are also located on the fiferail. The lifts, which are three-fold tackles, are easy to identify. The course clew-garnet is immediately forward of the lift; the remaining course lines are immediately aft of it.

Staysail downhauls are located on the aft side of the fiferails. Headsail downhauls are located forward on the dograil. Headsail sheets lead to athwartship pinrails, called monkey rails, on the forecastle. The staysail sheets are rigged to eyes on deck immediately below their pins on the pinrails. As mentioned before, they must be physically shifted from side to side when the ship comes through the wind.

The halyards are grouped together. By locating the upper topsail halyard, it is possible to locate the remaining halyards on the fore and the main. On both masts this halyard has the largest line and biggest purchase. It is located on the port side of the fore pinrail and the starboard side of the

Figure 14. Pinrail
diagram waist, forward

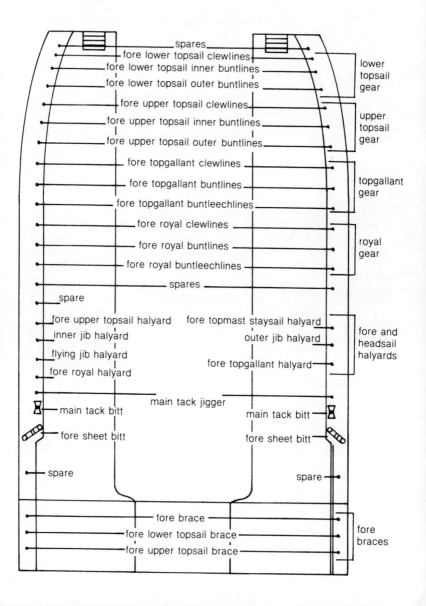

spares

fore lower topsail clewlines

fore lower topsail inner buntlines

fore lower topsail outer buntlines
} lower topsail gear

fore upper topsail clewlines

fore upper topsail inner buntlines

fore upper topsail outer buntlines
} upper topsail gear

fore topgallant clewlines

fore topgallant buntlines

fore topgallant buntleechlines
} topgallant gear

fore royal clewlines

fore royal buntlines

fore royal buntleechlines
} royal gear

spares

spare

fore upper topsail halyard   fore topmast staysail halyard

inner jib halyard   outer jib halyard

flying jib halyard

fore royal halyard   fore topgallant halyard
} fore and headsail halyards

main tack jigger

main tack bitt   main tack bitt

fore sheet bitt   fore sheet bitt

spare   spare

fore brace

fore lower topsail brace

fore upper topsail brace
} fore braces

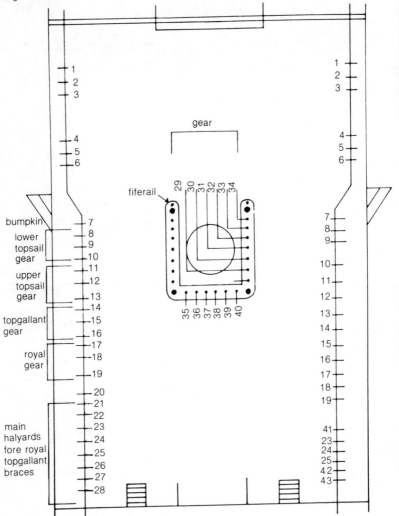

Figure 15. Pinrail diagram waist, aft

main pinrail so that the cadets setting the topsails will not interfere with each other when hauling on the halyards. On the opposite rail, further aft and with slightly smaller tackles and lines, are the topgallant halyards. Finally, alternating again to the original side are the royal halyards with the smallest purchases. They are placed farthest aft. Once the square sail halyards are learned, it is easy to locate the headsail or staysail halyards. Thus, directly opposite the upper topsail halyard are the topmast staysail halyards. Opposite the main topgallant and royal halyards are the main topgallant staysail and royal staysail halyards respectively. On the fore, the headsail halyards alternate back and forth. Opposite but slightly aft of the topmast staysail halyard is the inner jib halyard. The outer jib halyard is immediately aft of the topmast

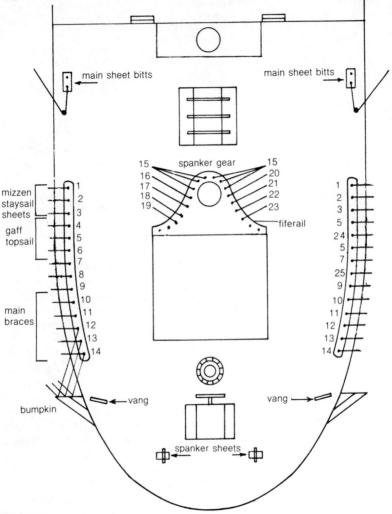

Figure 16. Pinrail diagram mizzenmast

main sheet bitts

main sheet bitts

spanker gear

mizzen staysail sheets

gaff topsail

main braces

fiferail

vang

vang

bumpkin

spanker sheets

staysail halyard. Finally, the flying jib is immediately aft of the inner jib halyard. Thus, the headsail halyards alternate from starboard to port, the halyard to the higher sail being aft.

The halyards for the mizzen staysails and gaff topsail gear are located on the pinrails aft, except for that of the mizzen staysail, which is on the fiferail. All spanker gear except the sheets are located on the mizzen fiferail.

Special purpose tackles, such as the preventer for the spanker, the tack jiggers for the course, and *rattail Jiggers* used for sweating lines, are shackled as necessary to eyes on deck and belayed to appropriate pins, cleats, or bits. When not in use, they are overhauled and stowed on the *spider bands* on the fore and main or in the settee on the mizzen.

The accompanying diagrams (figures 13–16) should be used in learning line positions. Particular attention should be paid to the type of lines used, their size, and their leads. Again, if the functions of the lines are understood and the position of the most obvious lines memorized, it will be relatively easy to identify the remaining lines.

4. Setting, Dousing, and Furling Sail

The safety and efficiency of any vessel depends on the close teamwork of every crew member. Nowhere is this more the case than on a square-rigger. The failure of a single cadet to ease a line at the proper time can easily prevent the ship from tacking. Throwing off another line at the wrong time can just as easily injure or kill a shipmate. Perhaps in no other setting is the need for—and importance of—a well-ordered chain of command so apparent. Indeed, one of the most important reasons for training aboard a sailing ship is the opportunity given the cadets to organize personnel into a close-knit team responsive to the orders of the commanding officer. The consequences of the failure to organize properly and the great importance of every cadet in the chain of command are reinforced by the extra time and effort needed when an evolution fails. For example, if the ship misses stays (fails to tack), yards have to be rebraced, sails reset and sheeted home, and gear laid out anew. A ten-minute operation can easily grow into an hour's hard labor.

ORGANIZATION

Cadets fill all sailing billets from the top to the bottom of the chain of command. Each cadet in a supervisory position is supported by an officer or petty officer who acts as safety observer.

The chain of command for a sailing evolution starts with the cadet officer of the deck who acts as sailmaster under the direct supervision of the commissioned sailmaster and the commanding officer. He has the responsibility for the successful completion of the evolution. Immediately below the sailmaster are the three cadet mast captains, supported by the mast officers. The mast captains must assign upperclass cadets to act as supervisors in key positions. These positions depend on the evolution but generally include a cadet in charge of each pinrail and fiferail, the braces, the headsails, and the staysails. When problems arise it is usually in this intermediate level of command. In most evolutions it is impossible for the mast captain to observe every line. Yet, without proper supervision a minor problem with one line can easily become a major problem for the entire mast. The use of upperclass supervisors contracts the mast captain's span of control to a more manageable four or five cadets (rather than a dozen) and allows him to devote more time to the evolution as a whole. In general, these upperclass supervisors should remain at their stations throughout an evolution so that they are instantly ready to deal with problems.

Underclass cadets are an integral part of the chain of command, although they usually are not assigned to any specific lines in an evolution. Generally, the first cadet to reach a line is automatically in charge of that line. It is his responsibility to insure that the line is fully ready before he reports *"Manned and ready"* to his supervisor. Specifically, he must insure that the line is properly faked out for running or led clear for hauling and that a sufficient number of cadets have manned the line to accomplish the task. The number of cadets required usually depends on wind and sea conditions, so the upperclass must intelligently gauge conditions in order that the appropriate number of cadets will be assigned.

At the bottom of the chain are the remaining underclass cadets. Nevertheless, they are an essential part of the chain: the success or failure of the evolution often depends on the actions of a single underclass cadet. These cadets must carefully attend to their duty so that they don't miss a command or respond to the command given to another line or mast. Additionally, they must act as safety observers and report fouled lines and other problems to their supervisor.

At the start of a cruise, when all hands are unfamiliar with the evolutions, it is particularly important that the chain of command be used so that each supervisor's span of control is small enough to monitor the assigned cadets effectively. As the cruise goes on, the upperclass cadets in the intermediate supervisory levels act as safety observers who only give orders by exception, e.g., stepping in if a line is improperly manned or if a problem develops. Leadership by exception is leadership, in fact. It is typical of the organization of a warship in a high threat environment where the extra seconds used in passing commands down the chain may be fatal.

In either case, the chain of command is absolutely essential to successful sail evolutions. Specific suggestions on organization will be given for each evolution as it is discussed.

SAFETY

Going to sea always has been and remains inherently dangerous. Sailing a complex square-rigger can be particularly dangerous unless an attitude of safety consciousness is developed by every member of the crew. It is this attitude, more than any specific rules and regulations, that will insure the safety of the ship and its crew. For example, one must automatically make sure that doors are properly secured so that they will not swing out of control when the ship rolls or tacks and that portholes are properly dogged to prevent flooding. Particular attention must be paid to housekeeping: a tonic can left on deck can easily cause a bad fall if stepped on during a roll and a book or a sextant not secured can easily become a missile hazard. What might be harmless horseplay ashore becomes potentially dangerous skylarking at sea. In short, safety at sea is a way of life.

There are several safety rules that are particularly important on the *Eagle*.

1. Cadets should lay aloft only on the weather side. If a ratline carries away or the person loses his grip, the wind will blow him onto the shrouds instead of overboard.

2. When going aloft on the mizzen make sure that all radio transmitters in combat information center (CIC), the bridge, and the radio room are secured and that 'Man Aloft' signs have been posted.

3. When laying aloft, cadets should hold on to the shrouds rather than the ratlines. The ratlines, which are of light line, occasionally carry away even with the best of preventative maintenance.

4. Gear that can be dropped, possibly injuring someone, should not be brought aloft. Nametags, watches, hats, and the like must be left below. Gear that is brought aloft should be secured by a lanyard.

5. Linesmen's safety belts must be worn aloft at all times. Until aloft, the clip should be hooked into the belt so that it cannot foul. In going aloft, running rigging should never be used for support nor for hooking on with a safety belt since it may become slack. Standing rigging, jackstays, safety stays, and fixed pieces of gear should be used instead.

6. The traditional rule of one hand for the ship and one hand for yourself still applies, even with safety belts. When working, both feet should be on the footropes or flemish horses.

7. Cadets should not lay out onto the yards unless they are securely in their lifts and the braces are taut. If not, the whipping of the yards may throw a person off.

8. While unfurling, the upper topsail should not be thrown off the yard until the men have laid in from the lower topsail, in case the sail blows in the face of those working on the lower topsail yard.

9. Unless instructed otherwise, no one is allowed to sit or stand on the yards. If the sail is in its gear or set, it may fly up and knock the person off or, when furled, may blow out of its gaskets.

10. No one should work to leeward of headsails or staysails, for a sudden puff may knock him overboard.

11. On deck, cadets assigned to headsail and staysail sheets must be particularly careful to control the sheets when setting

and dousing. The blocks on the sheet, if not controlled, may easily gyrate and hit someone on deck; hence the name widowblock. For the mizzen staysails, it is usually necessary to assign a cadet to walk the sheets forward or back to prevent this gyration. Similarly, in setting staysails, the cadets on the downhauls first must ease the downhauls off slowly. If the downhauls are slacked suddenly, the weight of the sheet block is sufficient to make the downhaul run. The sheet block will then crash on the deck.

12. In working with lines, a sufficient number of cadets must be assigned according to wind conditions. Bad rope burns can easily occur if a line is undermanned, not to mention damage to the sails.

13. It is particularly important to keep hands away from blocks when hauling and to stand clear of bights. Such lines often run so fast that one can be caught without warning in the block or bight.

14. In all shipboard evolutions, and especially sailing evolutions, absolute silence must be maintained except for necessary commands and reports. Singing out when hauling around may sound "salty." However, in an environment where a score of different orders are being given at the same time, such singing can easily result in a missed command.

Overshadowing these individual safety rules is forehandedness: a trait possessed by all good seamen and absolutely necessary for an officer, standing watch. All hands must anticipate potential problems and take action to avoid them! Only through a forehanded appreciation of the inherent dangers of sailing and a strong spirit of safety consciousness can serious accidents be avoided.

SETTING SAIL

Although almost all of the 170-odd pieces of running rigging are used when setting and dousing sail on the *Eagle*, the process is actually quite simple. Once the sails are *in their gear*, a good crew can set all sail in less than five minutes and douse all sail in less than three. In contrast, an inexperienced crew may take well over an hour to set and douse.

The traditional order of setting square sails is from the bottom up, although the courses normally are set after the upper topsails; thus, lower topsail, upper topsail, course, topgallant, and royal. Headsails and staysails are similarly set from the lowest to the highest. Sails are doused in reverse order. This order of setting and dousing reflects the natural order of taking in sails as winds increase. Normally, royals, topgallants, and upper staysails are taken in first since they heel the ship excessively in high winds without adding significantly to speed. Courses are doused before topsails due to their large size and the relative difficulty in handling them. In light winds, all staysails or headsails may be set or doused at once. With a trained crew it is even possible to set two square sails at once.

It makes little difference whether square sails or fore-and-aft sails are set first. The officer of the deck, however, should make sure that sails are balanced among the three masts so that excessive helm will not be needed to hold course.

Before sails can be set, they must be unfurled. When furled, sails are held in place by gaskets which consist of a dacron strap with a manila pendant used to secure the gasket to the jackstays. When the sailmaster gives the order to set sail, the mast captain will give the command to "*Lay aloft and loose all* (or a given) *sail.*" Before cadets actually lay aloft, the mast captain must ensure that the braces are taut and that all yards are in their lifts. He should also ensure that all clewlines, buntlines, and leechlines are taut in case the sail "blooms out" unexpectedly when the gaskets are loosed and knocks a person from the yard or tears. With an inexperienced crew or when in marginal conditions, an upperclass yard captain should be assigned to supervise the unfurling aloft. When all gaskets are loosed, the yard captain (or mast captain) will give the command "*Let fall.*" On this command, the sail is pushed forward and off the yard and is then *in its gear.* It is particularly important that all gaskets be clear before putting the sail in its gear. If a gasket is missed, the weight of the sail will make it difficult to loose the gasket and may necessitate cutting it.

In light winds, when there is no rush, one cadet on each yardarm is sufficient to unfurl sail. They should throw off the gaskets as they work their way out to the end of the yards and then throw the sail into its gear as they work their way back in. This procedure cannot be used in strong winds since the sail may bloom out before all of the gaskets are clear and may jam the remaining gaskets. Moreover, with a single cadet on the yardarm, the sail will not be put into its gear all at once: it will slat around and possibly rip. Therefore, when in strong winds, or when speed is important, several cadets should be sent out on each yardarm so that all gaskets can be removed and the sail can be thrown in its gear simultaneously.

SETTING SQUARE SAILS

The first step in setting all square sails is *sheeting home,* or hauling the sail down to the next yard, like a window shade, by hauling on the sheets and easing the clewlines. Since the sheets are opposed by the clewlines and the bunt of the sail is held up by the buntlines and leechlines or bunt leechlines, these lines must be thrown off. On the courses, tacks and sheets are hauled, as appropriate, to position the sail immediately below the yard. Since there is no strain on the clewlines, buntlines, and leechlines, they can be left untended if they are properly faked out for running. However, if enough cadets are available, it is best to assign one to each pinrail to ensure that the lines run clear. Three cadets are usually sufficient to man each sheet, for the lower topsail is small and easily handled. Further, the yards of the upper three sails will be in their lifts and therefore their sails will not receive the full force of the wind. In strong winds it will probably be necessary to *marry* the sheets before belaying them to ensure that the leech of the sail remains taut. In sheeting home, the clew of the sail should *not* be hauled down into the sheet block of the lower yard since it will probably jam. Two or three links of the chain portion of the sheet should remain out of the block for the sail to be properly set.

The courses are a different matter, since they are the largest sails set. In light winds, three or four cadets will be sufficient to man the tacks and sheets which take a strain. In strong winds, ten or more cadets may be needed to do the same job and a *stopper* will have to be passed so that the line may be safely belayed. Common sense is called for in manning course tacks and sheets. When braced up hard, all the strain will be on the weather tack and lee sheet; individual cadets can handle the remaining tack and sheet. When braced square, both sheets will have to be manned equally, with a single cadet tending each tack. When braced anywhere between these two points, most cadets should be stationed at the weather tack and lee sheet, but several will be needed at the other two lines in order to adjust the sail to lie directly beneath the yard. (See figure 17.)

The sequence of commands in setting the lower topsails and in the first stage of setting the other sails is as following:

1. Manning:

a. Mast captain: *"Man the lower topsail* (as appropriate) *gear."*

b. Upperclass supervisors in charge of the pinrails and fiferails will have underclass cadets man the clewlines, buntlines, leechlines or bunt-leechlines, sheets, and on the courses, tacks. The first cadet to reach a line is in charge of that line. When his line is rigged for running or hauling, and is properly manned, he will report to his supervisor *"Line manned and ready."* The upperclass will submit a consolidated report

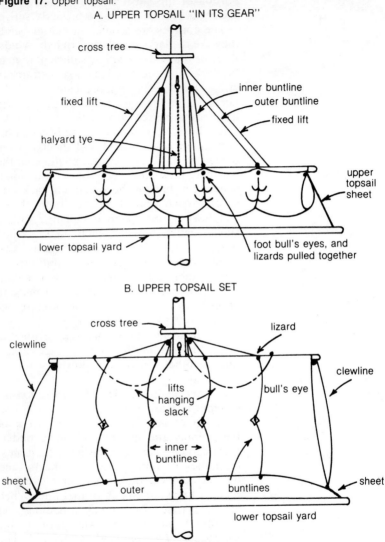

Figure 17. Upper topsail.

A. UPPER TOPSAIL "IN ITS GEAR"

cross tree

inner buntline

outer buntline

fixed lift

fixed lift

halyard tye

upper topsail sheet

lower topsail yard

foot bull's eyes, and lizards pulled together

B. UPPER TOPSAIL SET

cross tree

lizard

clewline

clewline

lifts hanging slack

bull's eye

sheet

inner buntlines

outer

buntlines

sheet

lower topsail yard

to the mast captain: *"Port gear* (starboard, fiferail, etc.) *manned and ready."*

2. Setting:

a. Mast captain to supervisors: *"Sheet home the lower topsail. Belay."*

b. Pinrail supervisors: *"Throw off the buntlines, ease the clewlines."*

c. Fiferail supervisor: *"Haul around on the sheets."*

For the courses, the mast captain will designate which lines should be worked, rather than giving the command *"Sheet home."* For example: *"Haul around on the weather tack and lee sheet. Tend the lee tack and weather sheet."* When the yards are braced sharp, he will usually order the pinrail supervisor to *"Board the tack."* Cadets will then rig the tack jigger, which is stowed on the spider band, to the pendant from the clew of the sail and will haul the leech of the sail taut without further command.

To complete setting the upper three sails, it is necessary to walk away with the halyard while continuing to ease the clewlines with the buntlines, and bunt-leechlines still off the pin. However, it is critically important that the braces be eased and the sheets of the sail above be thrown off to prevent binding. As can be seen in figure 18, the braces form the hypotenuse of a right triangle whose sides are the deck and the mast. As the yard is raised, the hypotenuse grows longer. Unless the braces are eased, the yard will jam, or a brace or halyard will part. For this reason both upper topsail and—for reasons to be explained in the section on trimming—the lee brace of the topgallants and royals must be eased as the yard is raised.

Figure 18.

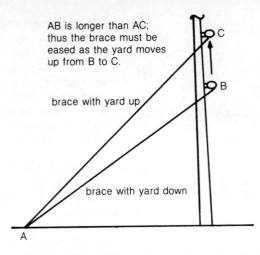

AB is longer than AC; thus the brace must be eased as the yard moves up from B to C.

brace with yard up

brace with yard down

As can be seen in figure 19, the sheets for a given sail are led along the yard below the one on which the sail is bent. As that yard is raised, the distance between *C* and *D* will increase and the sheet will pay out through the cloverleaf block at the center of the yard (*C*); the necessary slack will be taken up from the sheet at the yardarm (*A–B*). It might seem that what is lost at *A–B* is balanced by what is gained at *C–D*, so that no adjustment of the sheet would have to be made on deck, but this is not the case. Both *A–B* and *C–D* form the hypotenuses of right triangles. The lead of *A–B* is not quite vertical at the start; its angle increases if the yards are fanned. Similarly, the inboard block (*C*) is actually a foot or more forward of the mast. Thus, the sheet leads down at an angle which depends on how far the yards are braced around. As a result, the distance lost at *A–B* often may be less than that needed at *C–D* as the yard goes up.

Figure 19.

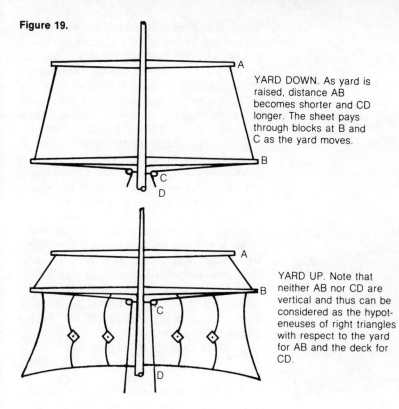

YARD DOWN. As yard is raised, distance AB becomes shorter and CD longer. The sheet pays through blocks at B and C as the yard moves.

YARD UP. Note that neither AB nor CD are vertical and thus can be considered as the hypoteneuses of right triangles with respect to the yard for AB and the deck for CD.

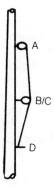

SIDE VIEW. Note that neither AB nor CD are vertical in a side view and can be seen as forming the hypoteneuse of right triangles. Thus, a complex situation is created in which the distance lost at AB as the yard rises may be less than the distance needed at BD to compensate for the yard rising. Since the leads of the sheets are complex, it is difficult to predict which will become taut. Thus, both sheets should be cast off before setting or dousing sail.

Thus, the sheet will bind. The leads of the sheets are geometrically complex, making it hard to predict which sheet will become taut at a given point of sailing. Therefore, it is best to throw them off *both when raising and lowering* a yard to prevent the sheets from binding and possibly parting. Since the upper sail will never be set at this time, there is no strain on the sheets and no danger in throwing them off.

Once the braces and sheets to the next sail (above) have been attended to, setting the sail is simple. The halyard is hauled up until the leeches are taut. (Normally, a tape marking will be placed on the backstay, along which the halyard block trolley rides, to indicate when the sail is properly set.) The sequence of commands are as follows:

1. Manning and sheeting home are the same as with the lower topsail. After all is manned and ready and sheets for the sail above have been thrown off:

a. Mast captain to supervisors: *"Sheet home the upper topsail* (topgallant, royal). *Belay."*

b. Pinrail supervisors: *"Throw off the buntlines and bunt-leechlines. Ease the clewlines."*

c. Fiferail supervisor: *"Haul around on the sheets."*

2. Raising the yard:

a. Mast captain to men on deck: *"Walk away with the halyard."* The upperclass supervisor in the area should stand near the halyard and act as a safety supervisor. Buntlines and bunt-leechlines are kept off the pin and run clear. Clewlines are eased out.

b. Mast captain to supervisor of braces: *"Ease the upper topsail braces"* or *"Ease the lee topgallant brace.*" The supervisor should order the cadets on the braces to ease off the braces enough so that the yard can go up easily but not so much as to allow a *catenary* to develop in the brace, which would allow the yard to swing out of control. He should also adjust the braces to provide an appropriate fan. What can be done easily by one cadet while setting the sails will take a dozen afterwards as the braces have to be hauled against the force of the wind.

c. Mast captain (when sail is almost set): *"Hand over hand the halyard. Belay."* Generally, it will be necessary to pass a stopper in order to belay the upper topsail halyard. The topgallant and royal halyards can usually be belayed by marrying the halyard *falls.* In marginal conditions or when only a few men are available, it is safer to pass a stopper.

After all square sails are set it may be necessary to *overhaul* the gear. The weight of the buntlines and leechlines, especially in light airs, may curl the foot of the sail or may not pay out completely when the sail is set. When overhauling, cadets should pull excess line aloft and through the lizards so that the sail will fill completely. In very light airs it may be necessary to use *rotten stuff* to stop off the lines. In such cases, it is important to use the minimum amount of line necessary so that the stops can be broken by a sharp tug from deck and cadets will not have to be sent aloft to clear away the stops when sails are to be doused.

SETTING HEADSAILS AND STAYSAILS

Staysails and headsails are easier to set than the square sails. Due to the danger of whipping blocks, however, they are potentially much more dangerous. Staysail sheets are normally not rigged when the sails are furled. Thus, the first step in setting staysails is to rig the sheets on the appropriate tack and to unfurl the sails. Particular care must be taken in rigging sheets since an error can easily result in a torn sail, even in moderate winds. Sheets must be led outboard of the stays and clear of the gantlines and other lines leading down the aft side of the mast. The sheet for a staysail is always rigged aft and outboard of the staysail below it. Headsail sheets are permanently rigged and are always ready for setting.

For setting, the downhauls are faked out for running and the halyard hauled until the luff of the sail is taut and no *scallops* are seen. Normally, at least four or five cadets are needed on a halyard although in high winds twice that number will be needed. If enough cadets are available, all headsails or staysails on a mast can be set simultaneously. As the sail is hauled up, the sheet should be tended and then sheeted home. If the sheet is hauled too tight, it will bind the hanks against the stay and make it difficult to set the sail; if the sheet is slacked the sail will slat around and may tear. Thus, careful attention is needed during the entire process. In light winds one or two cadets are needed on a sheet. In high winds three or four will be needed to tend the sheet and several more to sheet it home when the sail is all the way up the stay. Since headsails and staysails are particularly hard to handle in gusts, insufficient manning may easily result in bad rope burns. In high winds it may be necessary to use a rattail jigger to sweat the sheet home.

Sail trim will be discussed later. However, the sails must be trimmed in enough so that the sheet of an upper sail does not chafe against a lower sail since such chafing will quickly wear through the sail. Similarly, the wire rope pendant of the weather sheet on the headsails (which does not have any strain) will quickly chafe through if it is allowed to lie on the forward stays. Thus, after the headsails are set, the weather headsail sheet pendants and their blocks should be passed over the stays. As a result, the manila sheet, which can more easily stand the chafing will lie on the stay.

As mentioned in the section on safety, staysail sheets tend to gyrate if not carefully controlled when the sail is set or doused. As a result, all hands should stand well clear of the staysail (and headsail) blocks which are aptly called "widow makers." In particular, a cadet should be assigned to walk up each of the mizzen staysail sheets to protect the quarterdeck personnel.

The sequence of commands in setting headsails and staysails is as follows:

1. Mast captain (after all have been reported manned and ready): *"Ease the downhauls. Walk away with the halyard. Tend the sheets."* In complex evolutions like tacking, the mast captain may delegate the setting of the staysails to an upperclass supervisor, in which case he will merely say *"Set the staysail"* and will let the supervisor give the rest of the commands when all is ready.

2. Mast captain (when halyard is almost up): *"Hand over hand the halyard. Belay. Sheet home."* The pinrail supervisor will

then trim the sail by the sheets without any further command.

Setting the spanker is quite easy. The boom must first be topped about a foot and a half so that the sail can be set without damaging its leech and the preventer rigged on the lee side (the side opposite the wind). The boom is then positioned for setting by hauling on the preventer while easing the sheet, weather vang, and weather flag halyard. Normally, unless the ship is rolling heavily, three or four cadets will suffice for the preventer and one each for the remaining lines. Once the boom is out, the sail is set by hauling on the outhauls while easing the inhauls and brails. Since the spanker is one of the largest sails aboard the *Eagle*, quite a few cadets are needed to set it. A single cadet can handle all of the brails on each side; similarly, one cadet is sufficient for each inhaul. At least three cadets will be needed on the peak outhaul and five cadets on the foot outhaul, although more are preferable.

The sequence of commands is as follows:

1. Preliminary steps after sail is loosed. (All medium frequency and high frequency transmitters must be secured before sending men aloft on the mizzen.)

a. Mast captain: "*Rig the preventer. Man the spanker gear.*"

b. Mast captain (when all is ready): "*Haul away on the topping lift. Ease the sheet. Belay*" (when the boom is high enough for the sail to set properly, usually about a foot and a half).

c. Mast captain: "*Heave around on the*

preventer. Ease the sheet. Tend the vangs and flag halyards."

2. Setting the sail:

a. Mast captain: *"Ease the peak and foot inhauls and the brails. Haul away on the peak and foot outhauls."*

b. Mast captain (when all scallops have been removed from the head and foot): *"Belay."*

SETTING THE GAFF TOPSAIL

The gaff topsail is set much like a staysail: the halyard hauls the sail up while the sheet hauls the clew out to the end of the gaff. The clewline, like a downhaul, is eased. The tack is tended and then used to trim the luff and foot of the sail after the halyard and sheet have been belayed. Three or four cadets are sufficient for the halyard and sheet; a single cadet can handle the clewline and the sheet. The sequence of commands is as follows:

Mast captain: *"Ease the gaff topsail clewline. Haul around on the halyard. Sheet home. Tend the tack."*

DOUSING SAIL

Dousing Square Sails

The procedure for dousing a square sail is the reciprocal of that for setting it: those lines which were eased in setting are hauled upon, those lines that were hauled are now eased. The first step for the upper three sails is to ease the halyard to bring the yard down into its lifts and spill most of the wind from the sail. It might appear that the great weight of the yards and their sails would bring them down easily when the halyard is eased but this is often not the case. The entire force of the wind on the sail is concentrated on the yard shoe, which rides on a track on the forward side of the mast. This tremendous pressure, even in moderate winds, often binds the shoe against the track and prevents the yard from dropping. Thus, it is necessary to force the yard down using the only available lines, the clewlines. When the sail is sheeted home, they lead down to the next yard. On the command *"Clew down,"* the halyard is eased and clewlines hauled upon. The sheets for the sail above are thrown off to prevent any possible binding, and the braces, which were eased out in setting, are rounded in.

When the sail is firmly in its lift, it is necessary to complete dousing by hauling the sail up to the yard. On the command *"Clew up,"* sheets are eased and clewlines, buntlines, and bunt-leechlines are hauled until the sail is up. On the courses the process is the same except that tacks also must be eased and the command usually used is *"Rise tacks and sheets."* Obviously, the lower topsail, which is on a fixed yard, is merely clewed up for dousing.

A single cadet is sufficient to man the halyard, the sheets, and each brace. In light winds three cadets will be needed for each clewline and at least one for each buntline and bunt-leechline. On the courses and on other sails, more cadets must be added to each line as the winds increase, with the majority being added to the clewlines.

The sequence of commands is as follows:

1. Preparatory steps:

a. It is particularly important that the halyard and sheets be faked clear for running since a jam when the sail is half doused will result in the sail slatting around violently and possibly tearing.

b. The sheets for the sail above that being worked should be thrown off (in the case of the upper three sails).

c. The tack jigger must be cleared away on the courses.

2. Lowering the yards (upper three sails):

a. Mast captain: *"Clew down."*

b. Pinrail supervisor: *"Ease the halyard. Haul around on the clewlines."* Nothing is done with buntlines and bunt-leechlines. The man on the halyard must keep at least a half turn on the pin in case the halyard runs out of control and the yard crashes down into its lifts.

c. Brace supervisor: *"Round in on the (LEE) braces."* Braces should be carefully controlled so that the yard comes down *stacked* immediately above the course yard. What one or two cadets can do easily while the yard is dropping will take several cadets after the yard is in its lift.

3. Dousing the sail (all sails):

a. Mast captain: *"Clew up."* This command should be given as soon as the lifts come taut so that the cadets on the clewlines will continue hauling smoothly without a break. On the courses *"Rise tacks and sheets"* is usually used although *"Clew up"* is permissible.

b. Fiferail supervisor: "Ease the ——— sheets." Cadets must ease the sheets in a lively fashion since one cadet holding a sheet can easily check a half-dozen hauling on the clewlines.

c. Pinrail supervisor: *"Haul around on the clewlines, buntlines, and bunt-leechlines."*

The mast captain must carefully monitor the dousing of the sail and order *"Avast"* on each line as the sail is brought up to the yard. The lines usually come up at different rates and hauling on a line when the sail is already up may tear out the bull's eyes in the buntlines and bunt-leechlines or jam the clew block in the clewlines.

d. For the courses, the procedure is the same but the supervisors are different due to the different locations of the lines. Pinrail supervisors will order *"Ease tacks and sheets,"* while the fiferail supervisor will order *"Haul away on the clewgarnets, buntlines, and leechlines."*

After all hands have become familiar with dousing procedures, the mast captain may give the commands *"Clew down"* and *"Clew up"* to the underclass cadets on the lines without the intermediate commands by the various supervisors. The supervisors then act as safety observers, insuring that the proper lines are hauled and that the lines run free.

Dousing Headsails and Staysails

The headsails and staysails are doused easily by easing the halyard, tending the sheet, and walking away with the downhaul. The sheet must be handled carefully. If slacked, the sail will slat about and perhaps rip, and the sheet blocks will whip around dangerously. On the other hand, if the sheets are kept too tight, it will be difficult to haul the sail down. Moreover, the downhaul runs to the head of the sail, and then to the clew. In dousing, therefore, the halyard should be eased rather than slacked so that the downhaul will pull the clew up to the head of the sail and spill its wind. Obviously, careful control is needed throughout the operation.

A single cadet is needed for the halyards and sheets. As few as two or three cadets can handle the downhauls, although more are preferable to get the sail down quickly. Cadets should be assigned to walk down the sheets for the mizzen staysails in order to protect those working on the quarter-deck. If sufficient personnel are available, all staysails on a mast may be doused at once.

The commands for dousing are simple:

Mast captain: *"Ease the halyard. Tend the sheet. Walk away with the downhaul."*

Dousing the Spanker

Dousing the spanker is much like chewing up on a topsail: outhauls are eased, inhauls and brails hauled. After the sail is in, the boom is cradled and the preventer struck.

At least three cadets will be needed on the peak inhaul, five on the foot inhaul, and one for each brail. Due to the great size of the spanker, more cadets are preferred. The sequence of commands is as follows:

1. Dousing:

Mast captain: *"Ease the outhauls. Haul away on the inhauls and brails."*

2. Securing:

a. Mast captain: *"Ease the preventer. Tend the vangs and flag halyards. Haul away on the sheet."*

b. Mast captain (when the boom is amidship and the chock in place): *"Ease the topping lift. Haul away on the sheets."* and, if no sailing is to be done in the near future, *"Strike the preventer."*

Dousing the Gaff Topsail

The gaff topsail is doused much like a staysail. The halyard and sheet are eased and the clewline hauled. The tack usually has little strain on it and can be left untended. Two or three cadets are needed for the clew, and one each to tend the halyard and sheet. The commands are simple:

Mast captain: *"Ease the halyard and sheet. Haul away on the gaff topsail clewline."*

FURLING SAIL

In light airs it is permissible to leave the sails in their gear without furling. In stronger winds, the sails would slat around and quickly chafe; thus they must be furled. There are two types of furl: the sea furl, used when appearance is not a factor, and the harbor furl for when it is.

Sea Furling Square Sails

Furling is an art more easily learned from practice than described in a text. Figures 20–25 illustrate the proper way to furl a square sail. In heavy winds where there is danger of the sail ripping from slatting around, cadets should be stationed in the cross-trees and tops so that they may immediately lay out on the yardarm when sail is doused. In such conditions, the weather side of the sail must be smothered first so that gusts cannot catch the weather leech and cause the sail to bloom out of the hands of the cadets who are trying to furl it.

To achieve a tight furl, the sail must be completely clewed up to the yard. Care must be taken not to jam the clew in the clew block nor to pull the lizards for the buntlines and bunt-leechlines above the yard, where they will impede furling. The leech of the sail should be brought up parallel to the yard and held there until the last

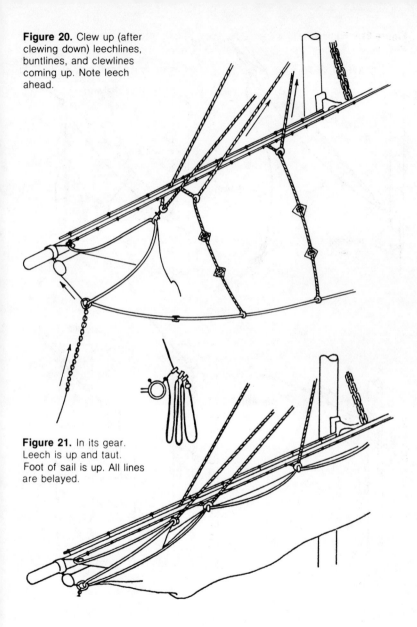

Figure 20. Clew up (after clewing down) leechlines, buntlines, and clewlines coming up. Note leech ahead.

Figure 21. In its gear. Leech is up and taut. Foot of sail is up. All lines are belayed.

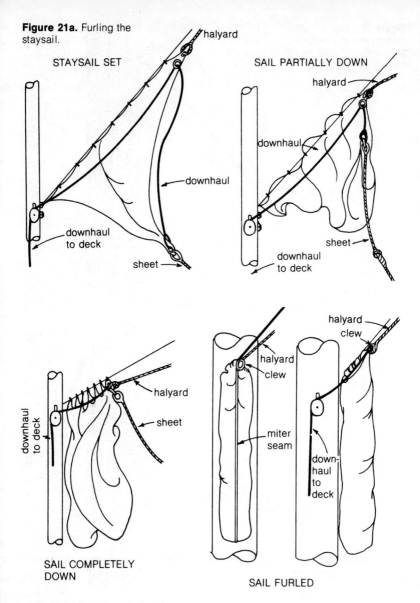

Figure 21a. Furling the staysail.

STAYSAIL SET

halyard

downhaul

downhaul to deck

sheet

SAIL PARTIALLY DOWN

halyard

downhaul

sheet

downhaul to deck

SAIL COMPLETELY DOWN

downhaul to deck

halyard

sheet

SAIL FURLED

halyard

clew

miter seam

halyard

clew

down-haul to deck

78/Setting, Dousing, and Furling Sail

bight is dropped (as shown in figure 20) in case an awkward tangle of sail, which is impossible to furl, is created at the leeches.

In furling, an arm's-length bight of sail is taken simultaneously by all cadets on the yard, is pulled up, and is held against the yard. As subsequent bights are taken, the earlier ones are dropped into it, until the entire sail has been taken up and the last few feet of the sail (at the head) form a tight skin. The entire sail is then rolled up on the yard and set between the jackstay and the safety stay. Gaskets should then be passed over the sail and secured to the safety stay. It is important that cadets not use any hitches that will jam in securing the gaskets, for it will be impossible to loose the gaskets without cutting. Preferably, a slippery clove hitch is used. Care must be taken that there are no *deadmen* and that gaskets are snug in case the sail works loose and blooms.

Harbor Furling Square Sails

When appearance is important, as in port, sails should be carefully harbor furled. The process is basically the same as sea furling but is more time consuming. The clew of the sail is brought up tight and the leech held against the yard. However, the foot of the sail is held against the yard and the buntlines eased out so that the sail hangs in a single large bight. Forearm-length bights are then taken and held, layer by layer, against the yard. The final bight is drawn tightly over the rest of the sail to form a smooth skin and the sail pulled up on the yard. After the sail has been furled, buntlines and leechlines may be stopped off to the mast to give a neater appearance.

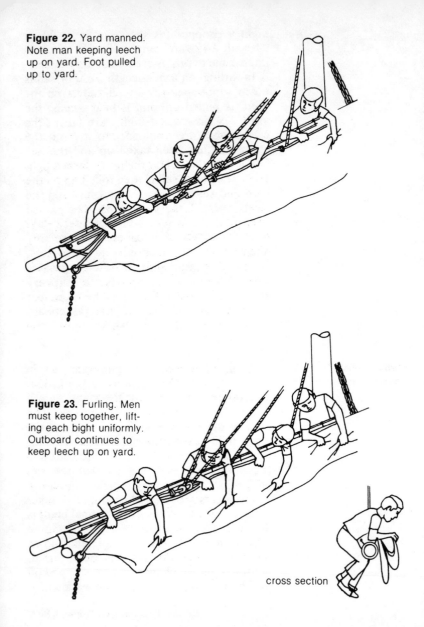

Figure 22. Yard manned. Note man keeping leech up on yard. Foot pulled up to yard.

Figure 23. Furling. Men must keep together, lifting each bight uniformly. Outboard continues to keep leech up on yard.

cross section

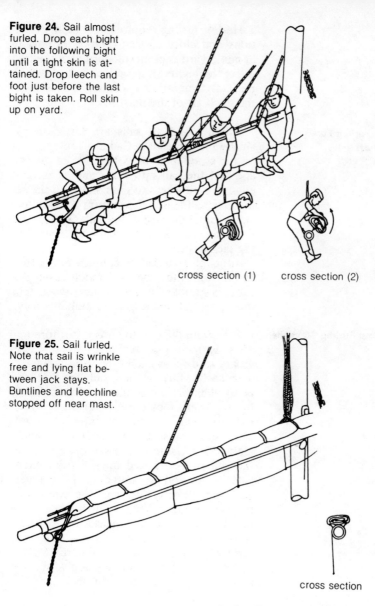

Figure 24. Sail almost furled. Drop each bight into the following bight until a tight skin is attained. Drop leech and foot just before the last bight is taken. Roll skin up on yard.

cross section (1)   cross section (2)

Figure 25. Sail furled. Note that sail is wrinkle free and lying flat between jack stays. Buntlines and leechline stopped off near mast.

cross section

Setting, Dousing, and Furling Sail/81

Harbor furling requires near-calm conditions and close coordination. It is best to assign a yard captain to coordinate the taking of the bights. A good harbor furl will be perfectly smooth and will not be seen from the deck aft of the mast.

Sea Furling Fore and Aft Sails

All fore and aft sails are furled in basically the same way. Cadets should lay out on the crane lines on either side of the sail and furl the sail into itself until it is tight enough for gaskets to pass and until the remaining sail material can form a protective skin around the rest of the sail. Gaskets are then passed around the sail and secured to the jackstays.

Although two cadets can sea furl a fore and aft sail, the process is much easier if a cadet is stationed on each crane-line so that the whole sail can be furled simultaneously.

Harbor Furling Staysails

It is more difficult to harbor furl fore and aft sails than to sea furl them and it is necessary to discuss each type separately.

In harbor furling a staysail, the first step is to shake the sail out so that it hangs freely. Then, locate the miter seam which runs from the clew to the center of the luff. The seam must be positioned vertically along the aft side of the sail. The body of the sail is then furled inward from either side. At the end, the miter seam is still vertical and directly aft, and the entire sail forms a smooth cylinder. The bottom of the furl should be neatly squared off. Gaskets should not be pulled so tightly as to disturb the tube shape of the furl. Figure 26 illustrates the sequence of dousing a staysail and its appearance when doused.

Harbor Furling the Headsails

Headsails are *french furled* in port. When doused, these sails are so bulky that it is impossible to achieve a smooth furl with them lying against the bowsprit jackstays. Therefore, the sail is hauled up about five or six feet, by means of the halyard, until the sail has been elongated enough to allow furling. The sail is then turned in on itself, as in furling a staysail, until only a tight outer skin can be seen. *Small stuff* is used to stop off that part of the sail above the jackstay. The resulting furl should curve down from the halyard like a banana.

Furling the Spanker and Gaff Topsail

The spanker is harbor furled exactly like a staysail except that there is no miter seam. A good furl resembles a tight cylinder. Since the foot of the sail is longer than the peak, there will be excess material at the boom. This material should be tucked in neatly so that only a tight skin can be seen.

The gaff topsail is an awkward sail to harbor furl. Like the spanker, it is bulkier at the bottom. The sail should be tucked in so that a tight outer skin remains and so that as little sail as possible can be seen on deck.

5. Trimming Sail

The *Eagle* is completely dependent on the wind, so proper trimming of the sails is critically important if she is to make her best progress. Square sails are trimmed by braces and lifts; fore-and-aft sails are trimmed by their sheets. Before discussing trimming, it will be necessary to explain the mechanics of bracing the yards.

Bracing with Sails Furled

Due to the number of other lines that are affected when the yards are moved, bracing is a little more complicated than merely hauling on the braces on one side and easing them on the other. In general, the buntlines, leechlines, bunt-leechlines, and, to a lesser extent, the sheets and clewlines will become taut on the side of the yard which is to be braced forward (new weather side) and will become slack on the side which is to be braced aft (new lee side). If the lines are not properly handled, they may part, the bull's eyes and lizards may be pulled out, or the sail may rip. The same effect is experienced by the lifts and results in the yards being *cockbilled*, or canted at an angle to the deck.

The reason for this problem can be seen by examining the case of the lifts in figure 26. The lifts lead from fittings at the side of the mast to a point on the yard a few feet from its end (figure 26c). When the yard is braced (to port, in this case), the yard pivots on the pin on the yard shoe (O) and the pin of the trusses of the lower two yards and the yardarms theoretically swing in a horizontal arc AB or A′B′. The lifts, however, pivot at their attachment on the *side* of the mast (at C and E) and can only swing in an arc AD or A′F′. If the yard swung around horizontally, the port lift could not reach its fitting on the yard, falling short by about the distance BD. Similarly, the starboard lift would extend beyond its fitting by the distance B′F, approximately, and would hang slack. Since the lifts of the upper three yards are not adjustable, the yard cannot

Figure 26.

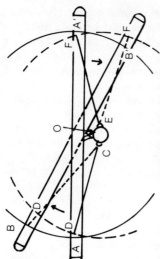

A. Front view, braced square.

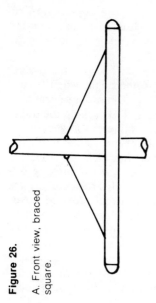

B. Front view, braced on port tack. Since lifts are not adjustable on the upper three yards AC = A'E and the yard cockbills upward on the weather side.

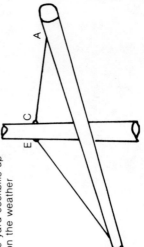

C. Top View, bracing toward port tack. The yard pivots at O, forward of the mast but the lifts pivot at C and E on the side of the mast. Note that if the yards could not swing upward lift CD could not reach its fitting on the yard at B as the port side of the yard swings forward and would actually reach only to D. Lift EF would be too long and would hang slack as the starboard side of the yard moves aft and would reach beyond its fitting at B' by the distance B'F. Since the lifts, except on the courses are not elastic nor adjustable the yardarm must rise on the side which is braced forward (here the port) and drop on the side which moves aft to compensate for the distance lost or gained as the yard swings.

actually swing in a horizontal arc from A to B. It is canted upwards, or cockbilled, as the port lift becomes taut (as shown in figure 26b). The opposite yard arm, then, cockbills downward and takes up the slack gained in the starboard lift.

The lifts on the courses are adjustable. It is possible, therefore, to have the yard swing horizontally by easing the lift on the side on which the yard is being braced forward (new weather side) and by hauling on the opposite lift (on the same side as the braces that are being hauled). Since the upper yards with their fixed lifts must cockbill as they are braced with sails furled, the sheet for the lower topsail (see figure 27) will become taut on the side on which the yard is being braced forward (weather) because the upper yards will be moving up as they cockbill while the course yard remains horizontal. Thus, it is necessary to ease this sheet and round in the slack on the opposite sheet.

In actual practice, the yards are kept cockbilled at the same angle when braced up with the sails furled, in order to present a neater appearance and to prevent the upper topsail yard from fouling the lower topsail yard as it cockbills. If the course yards are allowed to cockbill, the tack and sheet on the side on which the yard is moving forward (weather side) will grow taut as the yard cockbills upward and must be eased while the opposite tack and sheet must be rounded in. If the yards are not parallel after bracing, the lower topsail yard, which does not have a lift, can most easily be paralleled to the upper topsail yard by adjusting the sheets of the lower and upper topsails. In figure 27, the four sheets form two opposing pairs. The port yardarm can be raised by hauling on the port upper topsail sheet (a) and/or the starboard lower topsail sheet (b) while easing the port lower topsail sheet and the starboard upper topsail sheet (c and d). The course yards can be adjusted by throwing off the lower topsail sheets and adjusting the lifts.

Just as the lifts are affected by bracing, so too are the buntlines, bunt-leechlines, and

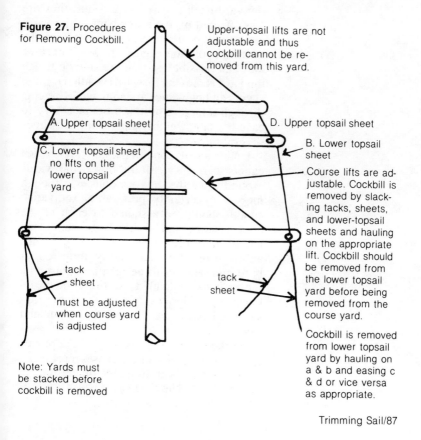

Figure 27. Procedures for Removing Cockbill.

Upper-topsail lifts are not adjustable and thus cockbill cannot be removed from this yard.

A. Upper topsail sheet

D. Upper topsail sheet

C. Lower topsail sheet no lifts on the lower topsail yard

B. Lower topsail sheet

Course lifts are adjustable. Cockbill is removed by slacking tacks, sheets, and lower-topsail sheets and hauling on the appropriate lift. Cockbill should be removed from the lower topsail yard before being removed from the course yard.

tack
sheet

tack
sheet

must be adjusted when course yard is adjusted

Cockbill is removed from lower topsail yard by hauling on a & b and easing c & d or vice versa as appropriate.

Note: Yards must be stacked before cockbill is removed

leechlines whose leads are approximately the same as the lifts. As the yard moves forward (weather side), the lines become taut and may part, pull out lizards or bull's eyes, or tear the sail, especially when the sails are harbor-furled. On the opposite (lee) side the lines will hang slack. Thus, in bracing, the lines on the side on which the yard is moving forward (weather side) must be taken off their pin or at least eased. Clewlines and sheets lead along the edge of the yard and pivot fairly closely to where the yard itself pivots. As a result, they are less affected by the movement of the yard. Nevertheless, if they are snug before the bracing evolution begins, they will become taut and possibly part on the side on which the yard is moving forward (weather). If the sheets and clewlines are snug while bracing through a large arc, it will be necessary to ease the new weather sheets and clewlines several inches.

Under ideal conditions, as few as ten cadets can successfully brace the yards around when the sails are doused, although more are certainly preferable. Individual cadets should be assigned to each of the course tacks and sheets. One cadet can handle all of the braces which are paid out, although one for each line is preferred. A bare minimum of three men is required on the side to be hauled for the course and lower topsail braces: two for the upper topsail, and one each for the topgallant and royal braces.

On the main, the proximity of the braces to the boat davits often causes problems. Unless handled carefully, the braces foul on the aft davit. The *timenoguy* is a whip running from the mizzen shrouds to the main brace and is used to raise brace clear of the davits. It may also be necessary to station a man with a special U-shaped boot hook near the davits to keep the braces clear.

The following is the sequence of commands for bracing:

1. Preparatory steps include laying out the appropriate braces, tacks, and sheets for running. All buntlines, buntleechlines, and leechlines on the side on which the yard is to move forward (new weather side) should be taken off the pin. The course lifts should also be removed from the pin. A cadet should be stationed by the clewlines and sheets to ease them off if they become too taut. When bracing sharp from one tack to another, clewlines and sheets will need to be eased about one foot.

2. Bracing around:

a. Mast captain: *Ease the ——— braces. Haul around on the ——— braces. Tend the course tacks and sheets.*"

b. Due to the differences in the purchases of the braces, the royals and topgallants will normally come around faster than the lower three yards. The mast captain can delegate the responsibility of keeping the yards moving around together to the upperclass in charge of the braces or he may give the order *"Easy on the ——— braces."*

c. If bracing square or bracing hard on a tack, the cadets easing the braces should pay them out until they reach their *leather*. These leathers consist of short strips of leather which are inserted in the brace after the braces have stretched out for the purpose of marking the proper position for the yard when it is square or braced sharp.

d. Once the yards are in position, all slack must be taken out of the braces before sending men aloft or before securing, in case the yards slam back and forth and possibly damage gear or cause cadets to lose their footing.

Bracing with Sails Set

Bracing the yards with the sails set is similar to bracing with sails furled. However, with the upper three yards up, the lifts hang slack. In figure 7b, all of the yards are tied together by the leeches of their sails. Thus, it is possible to adjust the cockbill of the yards by adjusting the moveable lifts on the course. In general, the yards should be kept parallel to the horizon to allow the best angle of attack of wind on the sails. However, when bracing with all sail set, the inertia of the tremendous weight of the gear will often result in the yards cockbilling, even if the course lifts are off their pins. For this reason, it is usually necessary to haul on the lifts on the side on which the braces are being hauled (old weather side or lee side) so that the yards can be kept parallel to the horizon. While the yards are in motion, two or three cadets can handily adjust the lifts; once the yards are set, twelve to fifteen will be needed to do the same job.

The wind usually strikes the sail at such an angle that the weather braces have more strain than the lee braces, so more personnel will be needed to brace when the sails are set than when the sails are doused. The extra cadets are assigned proportionately to the lines. If the courses remain set, it is particularly important to have sufficient personnel on the sheet that will be hauled.

It is also important that the cadets assigned to the tack and sheet (which have been eased out) pay particular attention in case the lines run away and cause severe rope burns. Similarly, those easing the braces must not lose control in case the yards slam up against the stays and carry away.

Before bracing from the sharp position, the tack jigger must be cleared away. Buntlines, bunt-leechlines, and leechlines must again be removed from their pins on the side on which the yard will move forward (weather side). If this is not done, the lines will curl up the foot of the sails and have to be overhauled. Sheets should be watched carefully in case they become too taut and jam in the sheet block at the end of the yardarm. Clewlines on the lee side will have to be eased about a foot as the yards are braced forward.

The commands for bracing with sails set are the same as when the sails are doused, except that *"Haul on the ——— lifts"* will be given as appropriate.

Trimming Square Sails

Theoretical Considerations

The combination of forces acting on the *Eagle* to propel her through the water is extremely complex and rather difficult to analyze. For purposes of trimming, however, only a few of these forces must be considered.

The wind that strikes the sails is not the *true wind* but a relative wind, a combination of the true wind and a wind vector produced by the ship's motion through the water. As diagrammed in figure 28, the relative wind is forward of the true wind. The faster the ship moves in relation to the true wind,

Figure 28. Wind and motion.

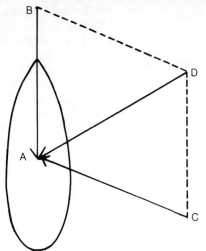

AB Motion of the ship creates a relative wind directly opposite to the direction of the ship's motion and equal to its speed.

AC The true wind.

AD The resultant relative wind experienced on board which strikes the sail. The stronger the relative wind AB the farther forward will be the resultant relative wind AD.

the farther forward the relative wind. The sails are always trimmed to this relative wind rather than the true wind. It is a fairly simple task since the ship's *anemometer* and all flags, pennants, and *telltales* indicate the relative rather than the true wind.

As seen in figure 29a, when the relative wind (AD) strikes a square sail, part of its energy (AE) can be considered as acting along the sail. This energy is not available for driving the ship. The rest of the wind's energy (AF) acts at right angles to the sail and propels the ship. Although present,

Figure 29. Relative wind.   A. The effect of the relative wind on the squaresails.

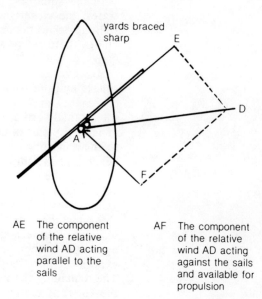

yards braced sharp

AE   The component of the relative wind AD acting parallel to the sails

AF   The component of the relative wind AD acting against the sails and available for propulsion

B. The relative energy of AF for different angles of the relative wind AD to the sails.

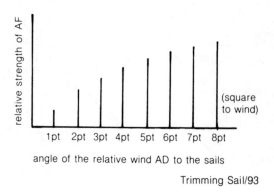

relative strength of AF

(square to wind)

1pt 2pt 3pt 4pt 5pt 6pt 7pt 8pt

angle of the relative wind AD to the sails

aerodynamic considerations are secondary with the square sails. As figure 29b illustrates, the closer the sails are to being at right angles to the apparent wind, the more energy there will be available for driving the ship.

However, unless the yards are braced square and the wind is dead aft, not all of the energy applied at right angles to the sails actually drives the ship forward. Thus, in figure 30, part of the energy (AF) applied to the sails presses at right angles to the heading of the ship. This force (AG) is opposed by the great resistance of the broadside hull to lateral motion through the water. However, as the ship can move sideways through the water, AG creates leeway. Furthermore, its force on the upper sails accounts for much of the heel experienced in moderate to high winds. The remaining energy (AH) actually creates the forward motion of the ship by over-

Figure 30. The effect of relative force AF on ship movement.

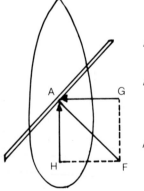

AF	The effective force of the wind on the Sails.
AG	The component of the effective wind acting laterally causing leeway and heel.
AH	The component of the effective wind driving the ship forward.

coming the much slighter opposing force of the water against the fore and aft cross section of the hull.

It should now be evident that trimming square sails consists of achieving the best compromise between (a) gaining the maximum effect of the relative wind by bracing the sails square to the wind and (b) applying the maximum energy to driving the ship forward by bracing the sails square to the ship.

Practical Trimming

Figure 31 represents the recommended angle of trim for the square sails. It was obtained by combining vectorially the concepts of figures 29 and 30 for all points of the wind. Yards are normally trimmed one point at a time, as shown in figure 31a. When braced sharp, the yards usually form an angle of about 45° or 4 points with the hull. At 90° to the hull they are braced square. The intermediate points are named by their distance forward of being braced square: square, one point on a starboard (port) tack; two points on a starboard tack; three points on a starboard tack, braced sharp. It is possible to brace the upper yards around to a greater degree than the course and lower yards. Bracing beyond 45° or 4 points, however, is usually not done. Beyond this position, most of the wind's energy is translated into leeway and heel rather than drive; thus, the marginal increase of speed possible is more than offset by the inefficiency created by excessive heel.

As can be seen in figure 31, the *Eagle* cannot point more than 5 points to the wind; even then she will be *pinching,* or not

Figure 31. Trimming the squaresails.

A. Positions of the yards when trimming squaresails.

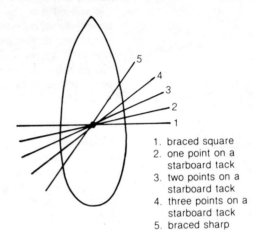

1. braced square
2. one point on a starboard tack
3. two points on a starboard tack
4. three points on a starboard tack
5. braced sharp

B. Theoretical optimum trim for squaresails. Theoretical speeds with wind on the quarters are not developed for reasons explained in text.

Relative wind	Best trim of yards	Angle of yards to wind	Relative force developed (scale of 10)
045 (broad on bow)	sharp	0	0
056 ¼ (3pts fwd of beam)	sharp	1 point	1.6
067 ½ (2pts fwd of beam)	sharp	2 points	2.8
078 ¾ (1pt fwd of beam)	sharp	3 points	4.0
090 (abeam)	sharp	4 points	5.0
101 ¼ (1pt aft the beam)	sharp–3 points	4–5 points	5.6
112 ½ (2pts aft the beam)	3 points	5 points	7.0
123 ¾ (3pts aft the beam)	2–3 points	5–6 points	7.6
135 (Broad on the quarter)	2 points	6 points	8.4
146 ¼ (3pts on quarter)	2 points	7 points	8.8
157 ½ (2pts on quarter)	1–2 points	7–8 points	9.2
168 ¾ (1pt on quarter)	1 point	8 points	9.5
180 (astern)	square	8 points	10.0

making a reasonable speed. As the wind draws aft, however, speed will rapidly increase. The yards should be left sharp until the wind draws aft of the beam and then slowly braced back until they are square when the wind is dead astern. Until they are astern, the yards will always form an acute angle with the wind. Besides developing maximum driving power, this will allow a smooth airflow across the sails and will minimize turbulence.

After the wind draws aft of the quarter, the theoretical driving power of the square sails will not be reached because the main square sails will *blanket* those on the fore. In the past the main course was often *goosewinged* in such circumstances to allow wind to pass through to the fore. Even now, when the wind draws aft, the main course should be doused to allow wind through to the fore and, in light airs, the sheets on the main square sails should be soft-sheeted— as long as the sails will not chafe on the stays—to allow even more wind to pass through.

The overall speed of the ship will drop soon after the wind has passed the beam, however, because the fore-and-aft sails will not draw to their best advantage. Furthermore, because these sails will not draw at all when the wind is aft, they must be doused. Their loss will more than offset the theoretical gain from the square sails. As a result, the best speed for the ship will occur on a beam reach.

If the sails are not set, the yards should still be trimmed. This is especially true when steaming into the wind, where there may be a difference of more than a half knot in speed depending on whether the yards are braced into the wind or boxed against it.

Cockbill and Fanning

There are two other elements that must be considered in trimming square sails: cockbill and fanning.

As the ship heels in a wind the yards will cockbill with respect to the horizon (the horizontal). As a result, the wind, which essentially travels parallel to the water's surface, will not strike the sails and flow smoothly off to leeward. Instead it will flow at an angle up and over the yards, causing an excessive amount of turbulence and a consequent drop in efficiency and speed. Thus, the yards must be trimmed parallel to the horizon. All sails can be adjusted at once by using the course lifts that are tied to the remaining yards through the leeches of the sails. In trimming the lifts, the lee course sheet and tack must be eased as the yard moves upward while the weather sheet and tack must be rounded in.

Fanning is the trimming process in which the weather sides of the yards are progressively braced farther back for each higher yard. The purpose of fanning is to allow each of the sails to present the optimum angle of attack to the wind. The true wind speed increases slowly with height above the water because of the lessening effects of the surface friction of the water. As the true wind increases with respect to ship's speed, the relative wind that strikes the sails draws aft. In other words, the relative wind that strikes the royal will be further aft than that which strikes the course. Fanning allows each sail to be properly set to the apparent wind *at its height*.

The upper sails are often fanned more than would be required for trimming because they act as a telltale to the officer of the deck and the helmsman. When braced back, they will begin to *lift* (luff) before the lower sails and thus will serve as a warning to trim sail or fall off before the ship is caught aback.

When braced sharp in light airs, the yards are fanned properly when each yard on the weather side can just be seen aft of the one below it when viewed from under the course yard. As the wind and heel increases, the fan should be progressively increased until there is a maximum difference of approximately a quarter of a point between each yard. Normally, yards are fanned only when the wind is forward of the beam. As the wind draws aft, the effects mentioned above become less important and eventually can be ignored. Thus, when the wind is more than a point aft of the beam, the yards are usually *stacked,* or positioned one right above the other.

TRIMMING FORE-AND-AFT SAILS

Although aerodynamic effects are important in understanding the driving power of square sails, this power is satisfactorily explained in terms of simple vector diagrams. In contrast, fore-and-aft sails derive the bulk of their power from aerodynamic lift. The fore-and-aft sail presents an aspect to the wind much like that of an airplane wing. The wind must flow more quickly across the curved leeward side than across the aerodynamically flat windward side (figure 32). In accordance with Bernoulli's principle, a low pressure area that pulls the sail

Figure 32. Lift.

A. Aircraft wing. The air must pass more quickly over the top of the wing than the bottom and thus the pressure is lowered and lift created.

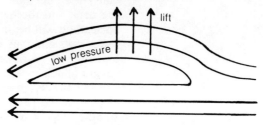

B. Staysail. Airflow is the same as with a wing and a low pressure area and lift is created on the back side of the sail.

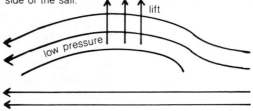

C. Slot effect. The inner jib forces more wind through the slot lowering pressure and increasing lift. The total lift with a proper slot exceeds that of both sails acting without a slot.

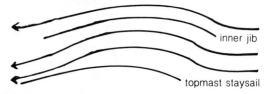

forward is created. The direction of this force, like that of a square sail, can be divided into an athwartships component which causes heel and leeway and a fore-and-aft component which drives the ship.

The close proximity of the headsails and staysails on each mast adds a second important factor: the slot effect. When trimmed properly, the sails will force the wind through the slot between the sails at a much faster rate than if the sails were separated. This greater speed lowers the pressure on the lee side of the sail and increases lift and drive. Thus, staysails and especially headsails must be carefully trimmed to each other as well as to the wind.

Fore-and-aft sails can be trimmed closer to the center line than square sails. Thus, when schooning it is possible to sail up to about 4 points off the wind before pinching. Under ideal conditions the *Eagle* can make up to 8 knots with just fore-and-aft sails.

In general, all fore-and-aft sails are trimmed just as the same type of sail on a small boat would be trimmed. Most of the driving force of the sail is created in the first few feet aft of the luff, so it is particularly important that the halyards be hauled taut in order that the luff has no scallops that would interfere with the airflow. The sail should be eased out to the point where it begins to luff and sheeted in until it stops luffing. After all sails on a mast are trimmed to the wind, they should be adjusted so that they do not backwind each other and ruin the slot effect.

The spanker and gaff topsail are trimmed together in the same fashion as the other sails.

The headsails and the main staysails must also be trimmed in relationship to the square sails. For example, if they are trimmed in too tight, they will backwind the courses. The speed lost due to the increased turbulence will more than offset the speed gained by the headsails or staysails. In short, the effect of each sail on all others must be considered. A somewhat less than optimum trim of fore-and-aft sails may be required, therefore, to allow the square sails to draw properly and to give the best overall drive to the ship.

Sail Balance

As the *Eagle* moves through the water, numerous forces act upon her hull, superstructure, and rigging. There is a certain point on the ship called the center of rotation. If the forces acting forward of the point are in equilibrium with those acting aft of it, the ship will move forward in a straight line. The location of this point depends on several factors, including trim and wetted surface area, but it is usually found just forward of the mainmast. As can be seen in figure 33, the headsails and foresails are forward of the turning point, the main staysails are immediately over the turning point, while the remaining sails and the rudder are aft of the point. If the sail plan of the entire ship is not balanced carefully, there will be a greater wind force either forward or aft of the turning point. This force will create a turning moment which will throw the ship off course unless it is opposed by the rudder.

The rudder on the *Eagle* is very large. In addition to turning the ship, it also acts as a huge brake whose effect, due to the greater resistance of the water when compared to that of the air, can offset the driving power of several sails. Obviously, it is beneficial to carry as little rudder as possible. To do this, a balanced sail plan is necessary.

Balance is usually achieved through trimming individual sails. Those sails may not draw the wind at their best advantage, but will allow the ship to drive at maximum speed because of their balancing effect.

The spanker is particularly important in sail balance. As one of the largest sails and as the furthest aft, it creates a tremendous turning moment. As a result it often must be eased out far beyond its optimum point to prevent the need for an excessive weather helm (lee rudder). When the wind is on the quarter, it may even be necessary to douse the spanker. Again, it usually is found that the speed lost by dousing is more than compensated for by the lessening of the need to carry excessive rudder.

In actual practice, the sails are balanced so that a slight weather helm (lee rudder) is required. This insures that the ship will luff up into the wind and lose way in the event of a steering casualty or other similar problem.

Trimming sail on any sailing vessel is an art mastered only by long practice. Nevertheless, it is an art which *must* be mastered. Efficient trimming can make a difference of many miles during a watch. Attention to trimming develops a sense of wind and wave. This sense is indispensable for a seaman on any vessel, sail or power.

6. Working the Ship

Under square sails the *Eagle* can usually point to within six to seven points of the wind; under fore-and-aft sails alone she can come up to between four and five points. Whenever the ship's destination lies further upwind than she can sail, it is necessary to slowly work up to windward by zigzagging back and forth in a series of *tacks* or *boards*. The ship will gain as much distance upwind as possible on one tack, will come about and put the wind on the other side, and will continue to work upwind in the opposite direction until the destination is gained. Obviously, on a square-rigger this is a long and arduous process during which the ship may have to sail six miles and many more in heavy weather where leeway is excessive across the wind to gain a single mile upwind. Proper trim is critically important in making distance upwind. Equally important is the ability to come about with a minimum loss of time and distance to windward.

There are three basic methods of coming about: *tacking*, where the bow is brought through the wind; *wearing*, where the stern is brought through; and *boxhauling*, where elements of a tack and wear are combined to allow the ship to come about in a minimum amount of space. Tacking is the preferred method for several reasons. Because the ship turns up into the wind, it only has to swing through about twelve to fourteen points as opposed to the twenty points needed when bringing the stern through the wind in wearing. Furthermore, the sails continue to draw and drive the ship forward throughout most of the evolution. In wearing, the staysails and spanker are doused before the evolution begins and the foresails are blanketed by the main for much of the operation. As a result of these two differences, a tack can be done in half the time of a wear: eight minutes as com-

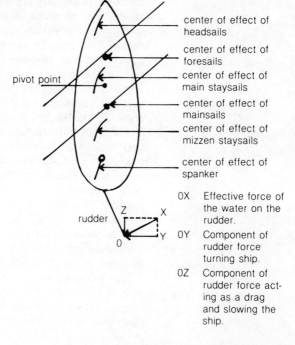

Figure 33. Turning moments around the pivot point.

center of effect of headsails

center of effect of foresails

pivot point

center of effect of main staysails

center of effect of mainsails

center of effect of mizzen staysails

center of effect of spanker

rudder

OX — Effective force of the water on the rudder.

OY — Component of rudder force turning ship.

OZ — Component of rudder force acting as a drag and slowing the ship.

pared to sixteen minutes, with a trained crew. If preparation time is included, the advantage of tacking is even more apparent. Most important, however, is that the ship actually gains distance upwind while tacking. In wearing, she falls off and loses some of the distance to windward which she so laboriously gained on the board.

There are situations where the ship cannot tack. In tacking, the foremast square sails are brought aback where they act as a huge brake. In light winds the ship may not have enough way to overcome this braking effect. By contrast, in higher winds it may be dangerous to put the square sails aback.

Because the masts are stayed primarily to offset wind pressure on the aft sides of the sails, only a few stays lead to the forward part of the masts to support them when the sails are aback. In general, the ship will not tack when making less than 5 knots and should not be tacked when making more than 12 knots (where the wind speed exceeds 25 knots). These speeds provide only a rule of thumb. In flat, calm seas the ship may tack at considerably less than 5 knots; in heavier seas she may miss stays even at 7 or 8 knots. Finally, tacking is an evolution where timing is critical. If only a small number of cadets is available, as with a single Ready Boat Crew, it will be necessary to wear rather than tack.

Boxhauling is used when it is necessary to come about in a minimum of space, as in a crowded harbor or confined channel. It may also be used to recover from an unsuccessful tack where the ship comes dead in the water before coming through the wind.

Tacking

Successful tacking requires a careful compromise among all of the forces affecting the ship. On the one hand, the ship should be sailed as close to the wind as possible to minimize the distance she has to swing to pass through the wind. On the other hand, the ship must be kept off enough so that she maintains sufficient speed to enable her to go through. Likewise, enough rudder must be used to bring the ship up, but excessive rudder must be avoided, as the braking effect of the rudder will slow the ship and may prevent her from coming through the wind. At all times the sails must be adjusted to help rather than hinder the swing of the ship.

The process of tacking is based upon common sense, once the forces involved are understood. As can be seen in figure 34,

Figure 34. Relative turning moments during a tack.

A. Full and by, with proper sail plan
A + B + C = D + E + F

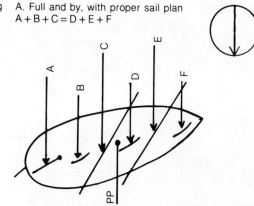

B. To turn upwind the spanker moment is increased by hauling it amidships. Headsail sheets are eased out to lessen the moment forward. Thus:

A + B + C is greater than D + E + F

The stern is pushed down and the bow is allowed to swing up into the wind even without the use of the rudder

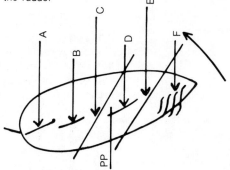

C. Head to the wind. The only turning moment is provided by foresails and rudder. The foresails will force the bow to port but only slowly. The staysails are normally doused and shifted at this time since they neither can drive nor twist the ship.

A   Turning moment of spanker
B   Turning moment of mizzen staysails
C   Turning moment of mainsails
D   Turning moment of main staysails
E   Turning moment of foresails
F   Turning moment of headsails
PP Pivot point

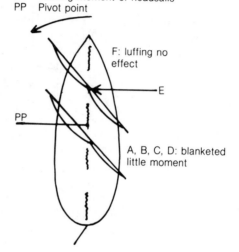

F: luffing no effect

E

PP

A, B, C, D: blanketed little moment

the headsails and spanker are the furthest from the pivot point and have the greatest effect in turning the ship except when she is head to the wind, where only the headsails will be effective in providing a turning moment. These, then, will be the most critical sails to handle during the tack. With their great turning moment, they can turn the ship into the wind even without the rudder. This capability must be used to advantage. The more rudder put on, the faster the ship

D. Through the wind before "Let go and haul."
Sails trimmed for maximum turning moment:
A + B + C is less than D + E + F by a large amount
and the ship falls off rapidly.

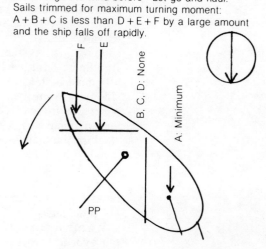

E. After "Let go and haul." Forces are about equal
around the pivot point so that after trimming
minimum rudder is needed.

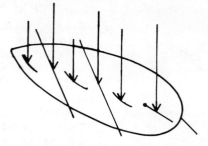

will turn, although the rudder will act as a
brake. It has been found that this braking
effect more than offsets any possible gain
from a quicker turn. Thus, it is necessary to
bring the rudder around slowly and add to
the turning moment by adjusting the sails.

Before tacking, all gear must be carefully

laid out. A jammed brace, for example, can cause the ship to miss stays. A jammed halyard may result in a torn sail. Staysail halyards and sheets must be faked out for running just as the lee braces must be. Buntlines, bunt-leechlines, leechlines, and lifts must be taken off their pins on the lee side to prevent them from coming taut and parting as the yards are braced. Lee clewlines may have to be eased. If there is some slack in the clewlines, they can be left belayed. The tack jiggers must be cleared away. The ship should be headed *full and by* with all sails drawing well, but she should be as far up into the wind as possible without pinching.

When all is ready, the rudder is slowly put over to start the turn upwind. Simultaneously, the spanker is hauled amidships to force the stern downwind while the headsail sheets are eased out until the sails no longer draw. This will allow the bow to swing upwind. The remaining sails are kept drawing to drive the ship forward.

As the ship turns into the wind, the square sails will eventually start to lift (luff) and will be ineffective. At this point the main course is brought up into its gear. This is done for three reasons: (1) if left set, it would quickly back and, being the largest sail on board, would act as a huge brake; (2) the leads of its sheets and tacks are extremely long, so it is very difficult to handle when bracing and the men used to handle it could more effectively be used elsewhere; and (3), by bringing the sail up into its gear, the sail master has a clear view forward and can more easily control the evolution.

While the main course is being put in its

gear, the main and mizzen staysails are doused. This is done at the same time as a matter of convenience. These sails will still be filling but not to their best advantage; they can easily be spared. It is easier to douse them when they are slightly filled than when they are luffing violently. This enables a small number of cadets to shift their sheets to the new tack and to have them ready to reset by the time the ship is through the wind, reducing the overall time for completion of the maneuver. Finally, and most importantly, the cadets are available: within a short time, all will be engaged in hauling on the braces.

The mainsail is hauled into its gear when it begins to luff. As the ship turns, the upper sails on the main will begin to back within a few seconds. At this time, the command *"Mainsail haul"* is given and the main yards are hauled around to the new tack. This action is the most critical of the entire evolution: if the command is not given at the right time, the ship will not make it through the wind. If the yards are hauled around too soon, much of the mainsail area, which would otherwise be blanketed by the fore, will be fully exposed to the wind and act as a brake (see figure 35). If the command is given too late, the main yards will back along their entire width and a tremendous amount of force will be needed to haul them around. While they are coming around slowly, they will again tend to brake the ship. The proper time for the maneuver is when the weather edges of the mainsails begin to back while the rest of the sails are still blanketed by the fore. At this time the wind will force the yards around quickly. A minimum of effort will be needed by the

Figure 35. Timing for mainsail haul.

A. Given too soon, the main sails back and act as a brake stopping the ship.

B. Given too late, the main sails are blanketed by the fore. Wind passing under the foresails backs main along its entire width. Extra effort is needed to brace the yards.

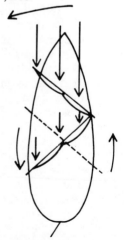

cadets on the braces once the initial inertia of the yards is overcome. The lee braces are eased rapidly out to their marks while the weather braces are hauled. The yards must be kept under control and must not run past their marks in case they slam up against the stays and cause damage. As the yards swing, there will be much slack in the lee braces and, when the wind swings the yard, even in the weather braces. This slack often fouls the boat davits. Thus, it is best to station a cadet on the boat deck with a U-shaped boat hook to fend off the braces and to have cadets ready to man the timenoguy in order to haul the main brace clear.

As the bow comes through the wind, the headsail sheets are shifted to help force the bow down or, if the ship has come dead in the water, are backed on the original tack to increase their turning moment. The spanker is eased off as far as possible so that it will no longer force the stern downwind and the rudder is put amidship.

The ship will continue to swing onto the new tack. When the mainsails begin to draw well, "*Let go and haul*" is given and the fore yards are braced to the new tack. As soon as it draws, the mainsail is set and, shortly after, the main and mizzen staysails. Unless otherwise ordered, all sails set on the old tack are reset on the new; if the tack was boarded on the old tack, it will be boarded on the new. All sails are trimmed to their best advantage without further order.

At times the ship will come dead in the water while heading into the wind. The ship will gain sternway very rapidly and the

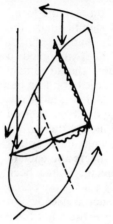

C. Given at the proper time, the wind backs only the weather edge of the main sails and forces the yards around. Only the wind passing under the foresails strikes the lee side of the mainsails.

rudder must be shifted in order to allow the bow to swing onto the new tack. Occasionally, the ship will not properly answer her helm in such conditions. She is then said to be *in irons*. In such circumstances it may be beneficial to douse the spanker in order to eliminate its tendency to keep the bow into the wind. If this is not successful, it may be possible to *chappel* the ship, a procedure which is described in Chapter 7. If the ship falls off onto the original tack, the yards must be rebraced, the staysails reset, and the speed built up in order to attempt another tack. If time is of the essence, it may be better to consider the unsuccessful tack as the first part of a boxhaul.

Organization and teamwork are critically important in tacking. Throughout the age of sail, crews of twenty men or less routinely tacked vessels much larger than the *Eagle*. The large complement of cadets on the *Eagle* allows a tack to be accomplished more expeditiously and with less individual effort. However, it requires closer supervision because of the relative inexperience of the underclass and because a single brace or halyard, improperly faked out and tended, may cause the ship to miss stays. While the division of effort among the cadets is subject to variation, the following organization has proven effective.

The foremast personnel should initially be divided between the headsail sheets and the main staysail downhauls. At least two cadets should be assigned to each sheet because the sails will luff violently when the sheets are eased. The fore personnel handle the main staysail downhauls because they are free during the first part of the evolution, whereas the main personnel will be busy with dousing the course and with laying aft to haul the main braces. As soon as the staysails are doused, the cadets can lay to their braces, fore course tacks, and sheets, and can stand by to brace the fore.

The main personnel should man the course gear, the halyards, and sheets for the main staysails. The cadets assigned to the course tacks and sheets should remain at their station throughout the evolution because the yards will be hauled almost immediately after the course has been doused and the sail will be reset shortly thereafter. Normally, a single cadet can handle each of the staysail halyards and sheets and each of the course tacks and sheets. It has been found beneficial to assign an upperclass cadet and two or three underclass cadets to shift the staysail gear once the sails have been doused. Working steadily, they can have all of the sails ready to set by the time the ship has passed through the wind. As a result, the loss of time and speed will be minimal. The on-watch Ready Boat Crew should man the main braces. If the yards are hauled at the right time, the wind will do all of the work. One cadet should be assigned to stand by with the U-shaped boat hook to fend the braces off the boat davits. After the course has been doused, the main personnel should lay back to the braces to assist in case the wind does not blow the yards all the way around.

Mizzen personnel should man both the mizzen staysail gear and the spanker sheets and vangs. The spanker is hauled up against

Figure 36. Tacking.

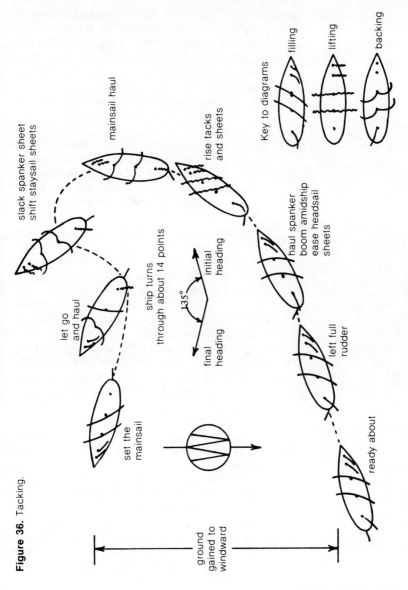

slack spanker sheet
shift staysail sheets

mainsail haul

rise tacks
and sheets

let go
and haul

ship turns
through about 14 points

initial
heading

135°

final
heading

set the
mainsail

haul spanker
boom amidship
ease headsail
sheets

left full
rudder

ready about

ground
gained to
windward

Key to diagrams

filling

lifting

backing

the wind, so as many cadets as possible should be stationed on the spanker sheet and then sent forward to the staysail downhauls once the spanker has been boomed in. The signal watch should tend the flag halyards to prevent parting.

The sequence of commands for tacking (see figure 36) is as follows:

1. Preparatory steps:

a. Sailing master: *"Ready about."* This command indicates a tack is to be made.

b. Mast captains: *"Fore* (main, mizzen) *manned and ready."* This report should not be given until all lines that will run have been faked out, all buntlines, buntleechlines, and leechlines have been taken off their pins on the lee side, and all personnel have manned their lines and are ready.

2. Bringing ship to wind:

a. Sailing master: *"Helm's alee"* or *"Hard alee."* This is an informational command notifying all personnel that the maneuver has begun.

b. Sailing master to helm: *"Right(Left) full rudder."* The helmsman must bring the rudder around slowly to prevent excessive loss of speed from the braking effect of the rudder.

c. Sailing master to fore mast captain: *"Ease the headsail sheets."* This command is given immediately after the rudder command.

d. Sailing master to mizzen mast captain: *"Haul the spanker boom amidships."* The rudder command and the commands for the headsails and spanker should be given almost simultaneously. The mast captains then give the appropriate orders to their personnel to carry out the required actions.

3. Bracing the main:

a. Sailing master to main and mizzen mast captains: *"Rise tacks and sheets."* This command is given when the weather edges of the mainsails begin to lift. On this command the main mast captain douses the course and the main staysails and the mizzen mast captain douses the mizzen staysails. Note that there is no separate command from the sailing master concerning the staysails.

b. Sailing master to main mast captain: *"Mainsail haul."* This command should be given as soon as the weather edges of the main sails begin to back. It is the most critical command of the entire evolution.

4. Head to the wind:

a. Sailing master to fore mast captain: *"Shift the headsail sheets,"* or, if the ship has lost way and may not fall off, *"Lead aft the lee sheet"* in which case the headsails are reset flat on the *old* tack so that they will back and help swing the bow off onto the new tack.

b. Sailing master to mizzen mast captain: *"Ease the spanker."* The spanker must be eased out as far as possible so that it will not hold the head up into the wind.

c. The Sailing Master should give orders to the helm as appropriate. If the ship passes through the wind, the helm should be eased to prevent the ship from swinging too far off onto the new tack and losing ground down wind. If the ship comes dead in the water and then gains sternway, the helm should be shifted to aid the ship in backing around to the new tack.

5. On the new tack:

a. Sailing master to fore mast captain:

"Let go and haul." This is given when the mainsails begin to fill and drive the ship forward. The foreyards are braced quickly around to the new tack.

b. Sailing master to main and mizzen mast captain: *"Set the mainsail."* On this command the course is reset. Main mast and Fore mast captains reset staysails without further command.

c. After all sails are set, each mast captain trims his sails and fans his yards appropriately for the new tack.

WEARING SHIP

Wearing with a Full Crew

Compared to tacking, wearing is a leisurely operation which can be carried out even by the Ready Boat Crew. It has the disadvantages of being time-consuming, of requiring the loss of driving power from many of the sails during the wear, and of losing distance gained to windward on the board. Nevertheless, wearing is necessary in very high or very low winds and where insufficient personnel are available for a tack.

As in tacking, the sails must be used to their best advantage to assist the ship in turning. In wearing, where the ship is turning downwind, the procedure is the opposite of that for tacking: the spanker, gaff topsail, and staysails are doused, eliminating most of the wind force aft of the pivot point which would tend to keep the bow into the wind. The mainsail is doused to facilitate bracing the main and to let wind through to the foresails when the ship has turned downwind. As the ship turns downwind, the yards are braced perpendicular to the wind and are kept square to

Figure 37. Wearing ship: simultaneous bracing.

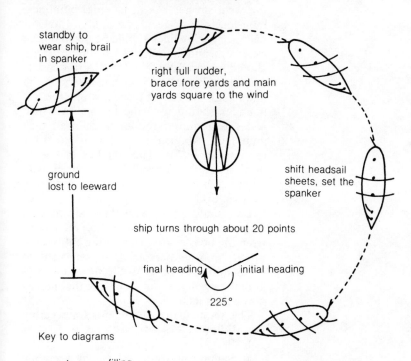

standby to
wear ship, brail
in spanker

right full rudder,
brace fore yards and main
yards square to the wind

shift headsail
sheets, set the
spanker

ground
lost to leeward

ship turns through about 20 points

final heading   initial heading

225°

Key to diagrams

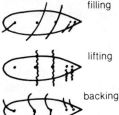

filling

lifting

backing

the wind until they are sharp on the new tack. As the stern passes through the wind, the headsail sheets are shifted but are not sheeted home in case they inhibit the turn back up into the wind. The spanker is set on the new tack. Its large turning moment will quickly force the stern downwind and pivot the bow up to the new tack. The staysails and mainsail are reset as soon as the yards have been braced sharp and all sails are trimmed for the new tack.

The organization for wearing is quite simple. The spanker, main course, and staysails are all doused before beginning the wear proper. As in tacking, buntlines, bunt-leechlines, leechlines, lifts, and, if necessary, clewlines should be taken off the lee pinrail and fiferail. All gear that is to run should be carefully faked out. A few cadets can be broken off to shift the sheets on the main and mizzen staysails while the remainder should man the braces. A single cadet is required for each mainsail tack and sheet. About three will be needed for each weather lift. The number of cadets needed for the foresail sheets varies with wind conditions but should not exceed four or five each. The on-watch Ready Boat Crew should assist with the main braces, again detailing a cadet to fend off the braces from the boat davits. During the entire evolution, mizzen personnel are engaged in booming the spanker to the new tack, rigging the preventer, and shifting the mizzen staysail sheets.

The sequence of commands for wearing is as follows:

1. Preparatory stage:

a. Sailing master: *"Stand by to wear ship."* Like *"Ready about"* in tacking, this command is informational and indicates that the ship is to be worn.

b. Mast captain: *"Manned and ready."* To be manned and ready for a wear requires that buntlines, bunt-leechlines, leechlines, and lifts are taken off the lee pinrails and fiferails, and all lee braces are faked out for running. Foremast personnel should man the headsail sheets and the fore braces, tacks, and sheets. Mainmast personnel must douse the main staysails and then man the course gear and main braces before reporting ready. Mizzen personnel must douse the mizzen staysails and the spanker before reporting. The Ready Boat Crew should assist with the main braces and provide a cadet to fend the braces off the boat davits.

c. Sailing master to main mast captain: *"Rise tacks and sheets."* The mainsail is doused for three reasons: the leads of the tacks and sheets are so long as to make the mainsail inconvenient to handle when the yards are braced; dousing the sail gives the sail master a clear view of the entire ship; and, most importantly, wind is allowed to flow onto the fore sails when the ship has turned downwind.

2. Turning off the wind:

a. Sailing master: *"Wear-o"*. This command is purely informational, indicating that the wear has begun.

b. Sailing master: *"Left (right) full rudder. Brace the yards square to the wind."* As the ship begins to turn, the fore and main mast captains have their personnel brace the yards to keep them drawing at their best advantage—square to the wind. The ship usually turns slowly, so the actual bracing is done a little bit at a time. Because of the difference in the purchases of the braces, the topgallants and royals tend to get ahead of the lower yards and must, therefore, be monitored carefully.

3. Passing through the wind:

a. Sailing master to fore mast captain: *"Shift the headsail sheets."* The sheets are shifted to the new tack but not sheeted home because they may impede the turn of the ship back upwind.

b. Sailing master to mizzen mast captain:

"*Set the spanker.*" Once set, the spanker accelerates the turn of the ship up to her course.

4. Reaching the new course:

a. Sailing master: "*Set the mainsail.*" This command is given as soon as the yards have been braced around to the new tack and the sail is filling properly. As in tacking, this command directs mast captains to reset the main and mizzen staysails.

b. As soon as the ship reaches her new course, the mast captains should trim their sails and fan their yards appropriately without further command.

**Wearing with
a Reduced Crew**

When wearing with a watch, the procedures (see Figure 38) are basically the same as when wearing with the full crew, except that the yards are braced progressively. The main yard is hauled around until it lifts. It continues to lift until it is braced sharp. This is done so that the force of the wind will not impede the bracing. It is important, however, not to brace the main around too quickly, for it may be caught aback, in which case it will cause the ship to lose way. After the main has been braced, the same procedure is used with the fore. The yards should be braced as soon as the foresails start lifting and, as with the main, they should lift until they are braced sharp on the new tack. Care must be taken, however, or they may be hauled too slowly, allowing the sails to be caught aback.

Obviously, with a small watch the maneuver is time-consuming, often lasting an entire watch. It is usually necessary to turn downwind very gradually and then run before the wind so that the headsail sheets can

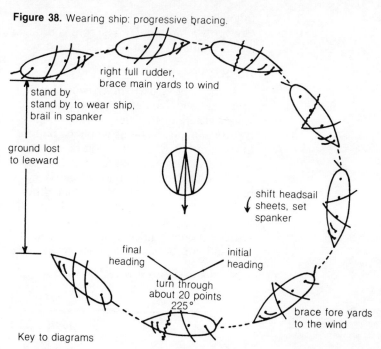

Figure 38. Wearing ship: progressive bracing.

stand by
stand by to wear ship,
brail in spanker

right full rudder,
brace main yards to wind

ground lost
to leeward

shift headsail
sheets, set
spanker

final
heading

initial
heading

turn through
about 20 points
225°

brace fore yards
to the wind

Key to diagrams

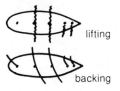

filling

lifting

backing

be shifted, the spanker set, and main braces remanned before continuing onto the new tack. The evolution should only be attempted when speed and distance are *not* important considerations.

The commands for a progressive wear are exactly the same as for a simultaneous wear, with one exception: the sail master, instead of ordering, "*Brace the yards square to the wind*," will order "*Brace the main yards to the wind*." At this command the yards are hauled until they lift and then will continue lifting as the ship turns. When the main has been braced to the new tack and the foresail weather leeches start to lift, the following command is given: *"Brace the fore yards to the wind."* The fore is brought around until it is sharp on the new tack.

Boxhauling

Boxhauling is used in crowded anchorages, narrow channels, and other confined waters where obstructions make it impossible to *headreach* as far as would be required in tacking but where the loss of ground in wearing is not acceptable. The evolution combines a tack and a wear and is more involved and time-consuming than either.

The first part of the maneuver is exactly like a tack. The rudder is put over, the spanker boom hauled amidships, and the headsail sheets eased in order to turn the

Figure 39. Situation requiring a boxhaul: working up a river.

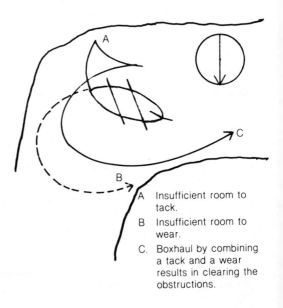

A Insufficient room to tack.

B Insufficient room to wear.

C Boxhaul by combining a tack and a wear results in clearing the obstructions.

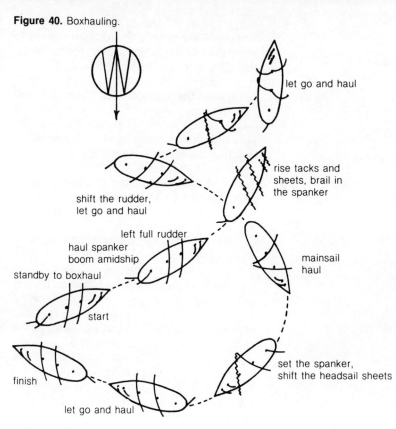

Figure 40. Boxhauling.

let go and haul

rise tacks and
sheets, brail in
the spanker

shift the rudder,
let go and haul

left full rudder

haul spanker
boom amidship

mainsail
haul

standby to boxhaul

start

set the spanker,
shift the headsail sheets

finish

let go and haul

Key to diagrams:

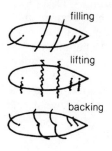

filling

lifting

backing

ship rapidly up into the wind. When the mainsails begin to lift, *"Rise tacks and sheets"* is given and, as in tacking, the main and mizzen staysails are doused. Unlike tacking, the spanker is brailed in because it is being blanketed by the mainsails and will not be needed in the second half of the evolution. Before the ship comes completely into the wind, *"Let go and haul"* is given, rather than *"Mainsail haul,"* and the foreyards are *boxed,* or trimmed square to the wind. When boxed, they rapidly brake the ship. Because they are braced onto the opposite tack, they tend to force the bow back onto the original tack. The ship will gain sternway very rapidly and will swing back. As the ship swings, it may be desirable to brace the mainyards to the wind so that they do not draw and oppose the backing effect of the fore.

The second part of the evolution begins when the wind has drawn abeam. Both the fore and main are braced so that they fill. As the ship forges ahead, a normal wear is conducted either by bracing simultaneously or, as in the diagram, progressively. If done correctly, the distance gained upwind during the tacking portion of the maneuver offsets most of the distance normally lost in a wear, so that the ship should end just about where it began—but on the opposite tack.

The *Eagle* is rarely required to boxhaul in confined waters since it has its auxiliary engine available for assistance in maneuvering. However, boxhauling may be put to good use when the ship misses stays. If time or distance is a consideration in coming about when the ship comes dead in the water after the mainsail has been hauled, the fore should be boxed and the main yards braced to the wind to gain sternway. The rudder is shifted and the spanker brailed in. The ship should back up into the wind until the mainsails begin to fill on the original tack, at which time the ship should surge forward. She can then be worn around onto the new tack.

7. Shipboard Emergencies

"It appears to me that when an officer takes charge of the deck, his whole mind ought to be occupied with what he would do with the ship in any case of emergency that might take place with the sails that the ship is then under."[1] What was true for Captain Learclet of the Royal Navy in 1849 remains no less true today. When an emergency strikes, there is rarely enough time to think out a course of action. Forehandedness, therefore, is absolutely essential for any deck officer or cadet in a supervisory position. By anticipating possible emergencies, most of them can be avoided and the remainder can be handled quickly and safely. The proper response to an emergency depends on ever changing conditions of winds and seas, so these conditions must be reevaluated continually during a watch.

SAIL EMERGENCIES

Caught Aback

Perhaps the most common sail emergency is being caught aback. This occurs when the wind backs the square sails because of a sudden shift of the wind or the inattention of the helmsman and watch officer. In light airs the ship turns so slowly that it may be impossible to prevent being caught aback by a wind shift. Fortunately, being caught aback in such circumstances is usually more embarrassing than danger-

[1] William Woodward, ed., *Professional Recollections on Seamanship, Discipline, etc.*

ous. In high winds, however, being caught aback can easily result in torn sails; in extreme conditions, it can cause damage to the yards and rigging. Because the ship will rapidly lose way with the sails backing, speed is essential to recovery. Due to this loss of headway, much of the recovery action will depend on the proper handling of the sails.

1. Wind on the original tack to dead ahead:

a. The first step in all recovery maneuvers, unless the wind has shifted so far as to make it obvious that the procedure will not work, is to put the rudder over full to fall off. The spanker sheet should be eased out and, in light airs, brailed in to prevent it from holding the bow into the wind. If enough people are available, the headsail sheets can be hauled flat to provide more turning moment to force the bow downwind (figure 41).

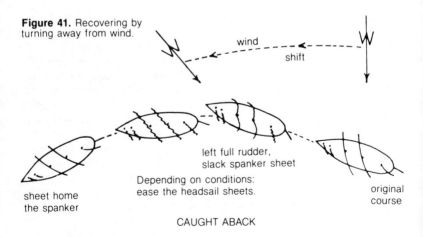

Figure 41. Recovering by turning away from wind.

wind
shift

left full rudder,
slack spanker sheet

Depending on conditions:
ease the headsail sheets.

sheet home
the spanker

original
course

CAUGHT ABACK

Figure 42. Recovery from wind shift.

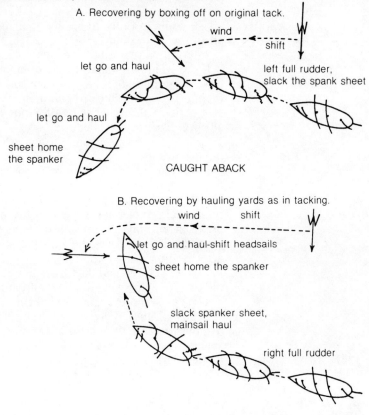

A. Recovering by boxing off on original tack.

wind
shift

let go and haul

left full rudder,
slack the spank sheet

let go and haul

sheet home
the spanker

CAUGHT ABACK

B. Recovering by hauling yards as in tacking.

wind   shift

let go and haul–shift headsails

sheet home the spanker

slack spanker sheet,
mainsail haul

right full rudder

b. If the ship comes dead in the water before the sails refill, the foreyards should be boxed so that the increased force of the wind backing the fore forces the bow down. When the ship has swung enough for the mainsails to fill, the foreyards are hauled again and the ship surges forward. If sternway is gained before the main fills, the rudder should be shifted to assist the stern in turning upwind. If the ship turns slowly, it may be necessary to douse the spanker and aft staysails in order to reduce their force aft of the pivot point.

2. Wind on opposite bow (figure 42a):

If the wind has shifted to the original lee bow and if full rudder has not been successful in bringing the ship around, more extensive action will be needed. All hands usually will have to be called.

a. If the wind has come around to the opposite bow, the ship has in essence tacked unintentionally. If there is no objection to sailing on the new tack, the ship recovers by hauling the braces as in an intentional tack. Tacks and sheets on the main are risen and staysails are doused as soon as possible. On the fore, the headsail sheets are eased or shifted appropriately. *"Mainsail haul"* is given and the fore is left on the old tack to help swing the bow off onto the new tack. When the mainsails begin to fill, *"Let go and haul"* is given. As the ship starts to move forward, the mainsail, staysails, and spanker are set and trimmed for the new tack (figure 42b).

b. If for some reason it is necessary to sail on the original tack, the ship may be *chapelled* (figure 43). In chapelling, the main yards are braced square, the spanker is brailed in, and the mainsail and staysails are doused. The fore, being braced sharp, forces the bow down to leeward on the new tack as do the headsails, whose sheets should be held so that they back. As the main is square, the *Eagle* will quickly build up sternway. As she gains sternway, the rudder is shifted and the ship swings its stern up into the wind. The mainsails even-

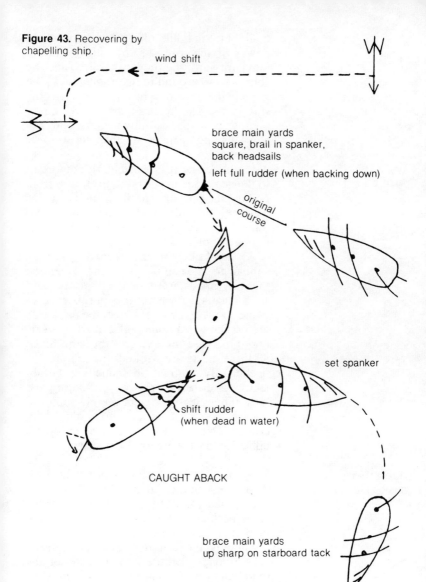

Figure 43. Recovering by chapelling ship.

wind shift

brace main yards
square, brail in spanker,
back headsails

left full rudder (when backing down)

original course

set spanker

shift rudder
(when dead in water)

CAUGHT ABACK

brace main yards
up sharp on starboard tack

tually lift and fill, offsetting the backing power of the fore. As the ship begins to move forward, the rudder is shifted and the ship is wore around to its original tack, the main being braced to best advantage as the ship turns. The headsail sheets are shifted as the bow passes downwind, and the staysails and spanker are then set to force the stern down.

In chapelling it is particularly important to douse the spanker first to prevent it from holding the bow up into the wind. Once this is done, the ship will come around, although more slowly, even if the main has not been braced square.

As should be evident, chapelling is very similar to boxhauling with the exception that the yards start off on the opposite tack. In boxhauling, where the purpose is to come about in the least space, the foreyards are braced when falling off and when wearing to increase the swing of the ship. Since all three masts are worked, the full crew is needed. By contrast, in chapelling the objective is merely to recover on the original tack. Thus, it is sufficient merely to douse the spanker and, if desired, square the course. This can be done, though with some difficulty, by the Ready Boat Crew.

Heavy Weather Sailing: Shortening Sail

Sailing in heavy weather is not in itself dangerous, but it can be if the watch on deck is not forehanded in anticipating possible problems. For this reason, it is included in this chapter.

There is always a tendency to keep sails set too long when the weather deteriorates (and conversely, not to reset them soon enough when the weather improves). In actuality, once the angle of heel exceeds around 15°, the increase of the wetted surface and the subsequent drag offset much of the extra drive of the wind. In particular, the royals and topgallants will do more to heel the ship than to drive it. In such instances, it is often found that dousing these upper sails has little or no effect on the speed of the ship, but it does improve the ride of the ship considerably. All in all, the decision to take in sail must depend on several factors, including the amount of sea room available, the condition and forecast condition of the wind and seas, and the experience level of the crew.

The order of dousing square sails is: royals, topgallants, courses, upper topsails, and lower topsails. In heavy weather, sails are normally doused and furled one at a time. If they are allowed to slat around in their gear, they may rip easily. Thus, cadets are usually stationed in the cross-trees and the tops before the evolution so that they can lay out onto the yardarm as soon as the sail is doused.

In heavy winds the yard shoes may bind on their track, even when the halyard is slack. Thus, it is important for the men aloft to make sure that the yards are in their lifts before they lay out. Similarly, if there is slack in the braces, the yards will swing violently. The mast captain must ensure that all slack is removed before allowing cadets out to furl. As usual, the slack created in the braces as the yards settle in their lifts should be rounded in on the lee side. The only exception would occur when rounding in on the lee side would result in the yards coming up against the backstays. The excessive pressure of the yard could damage the stay. In such cases, the slack will have to be taken from the weather side.

In furling in heavy weather, the strongest cadet should lay out to the windward yard-arm to smother the leech of the sail. Until the leech is in control, the wind will continually catch the sail and blow it from the hands of those attempting to furl it. Once the weather leech is controlled, the rest of the sail can be quickly smothered and furled, working from weather to leeward.

It may be beneficial to bring the ship up into the wind so that the sails begin to lift. This reduces the tendency of the sails to blow away from the cadets on the yard. On the other hand, the sails should not be brought aback in case they blow back on the cadets on the yards and possibly knock them from the footropes.

Staysails are doused from the top downward. Usually only a single sail at a time is doused in heavy weather to prevent slatting and possible tearing. With the staysails, it is particularly important that the sheet be kept under control to minimize slatting, and that the halyard be eased as rapidly as possible, but slowly enough that the downhaul pulls the clew of the sail up to the peak and spills its wind. In furling the staysail, cadets should work from the top down if there are not enough of them available to furl the entire sail at once, in case the wind catches the luff of the sail and causes it to blow out the lower gaskets.

Heaving To

As the winds and seas increase, a point is reached where the ship cannot make way without pounding into the seas or putting excessive strain on the rigging. If there is sea room in such cases, the ship can *scud,* i.e., run directly downwind and downseas. *Scudding,* however, requires close control to prevent the ship from swinging broadside into the trough and *broaching.* When in the trough, the great *tophamper* of the ship will result in wild rolling, which at its worst may part stays or even capsize the ship.

If scudding is not attempted, the ship must *heave to.* The purpose in heaving to is to have as little way on the ship as possible so that it rides up and over the seas rather than ploughing through them. The safest position for heaving to is with the winds and seas on the bow or on the quarter. A slightly smoother ride is provided with the seas on the quarter, although the rudder is more exposed to damage by the seas. Also, there is more of a tendency to broach when the seas are on the quarter.

Any number of combinations of sails may be used to heave to, although the lower topsails normally are used for the squares because they are the most easily handled, and the topmast staysails or mizzen staysail for the fore-and-aft-sails because they are low and have the least tendency to heel the ship.

In heaving to with the seas on the bow, the fore-topmast staysail, sheeted flat, can be used in combination with the main lower topsail, braced sharp, and the rudder lashed up. This arrangement causes the ship to slowly turn up into the wind until the lower topsail lifts, at which time the ship will lose way and the staysail will force the bow down to leeward until the topsail fills again.

During this time the ship may roll heavily but usually not dangerously.

When heaving to with the wind on the quarter, the fore lower topsail should be used to keep the bow well off and a mizzen staysail used to balance the ship and damp the rolling. In this case, much closer rudder control is needed to prevent broaching or allowing the seas to come dead astern, possibly *pooping* the ship.

The *Eagle* rolls heavily, regardless of how she heaves to. At times, waves will break aboard. Thus, the *heavy weather bill* must be set: lifelines are rigged on deck, all loose gear is lashed, and the maximum watertight integrity is maintained. Fortunately, the weather is rarely so severe as to require heaving to; when it is, however, a well-handled ship, when hove to, will ride moderately well.

Maneuvering in a Squall

Squalls are associated with the passage of weather fronts and with thunderstorms. In a squall there may be a sudden increase in wind speed—possibly up to hurricane force. Often this increase in speed is accompanied by a sudden windshift of up to 180° within a few minutes or even seconds. This combination of high winds and shifting direction can be extremely dangerous if the ship is under full sail and may catch her aback or *knock her down*.

Squalls can usually be detected both visually and on radar well before they strike. A prudent seaman will fall off and run before the squall. By running, the effective (apparent) wind speed is reduced by the speed of the ship. With the seas and wind astern, sails can be reduced with comparative ease. However, many squalls do not contain high winds; if the ship ran off from every one sighted, she would be hard pressed to meet her schedule. Thus, on occasion the ship will be caught before she can fall off or reduce sail. In such a situation, the ship will heel over excessively. The increased submergence of the lee bow increases its lateral resistance and tends to force the bow up into the wind. Unless quick action is taken on the helm, the ship may get caught aback. In any case, an excessive amount of weather helm (lee rudder) is needed to maintain course. Moreover, as the ship heels and the rudder becomes less vertical, its turning effect is lessened considerably. Thus, there is little residual helm available for falling off. Brailing in the spanker removes a tremendous force aft of the turning point as well as some of the heeling moment and thus allows the bow to fall off and the rudder to be eased. Nevertheless, an attempt to fall off may be dangerous since the ship will turn slowly. As the wind comes abeam, the heel may increase enough to knock her down. So, it may be necessary to ride the edge of the wind until the upper sails can be doused. Great care must be taken not to bring the wind too far forward in case the ship is caught aback nor too far aft in case she is knocked down. Normally, the extreme danger will have passed (even in a hurricane-force squall) once the royals, topgallants, and upper staysails have been doused.

If the ship gets caught with the wind abeam and the heel increases dangerously, the sheets for the upper square sails and staysails should be thrown off. This action can tear the sails, but it may save the ship by spilling the wind in those sails that add most to the heel.

The decision to fall off or ride the edge of the wind must be made according to circumstances. Only long practice at seamanship ensures the right decision. Obviously, the best solution is to avoid the problem, if possible, by falling off or by reducing sail before the squall hits.

Gear Carried Away

Great care is taken on the *Eagle* to prevent gear failure. Most of the running rigging is replaced yearly; the standing rigging, all blocks, and all fittings are continually inspected and repaired when necessary. Nevertheless, equipment casualties may occur in heavy weather. The general procedure when gear carries away is to remove the strain from the affected area and to secure the gear from thrashing about so that repairs can be made.

1. Running gear carried away:

a. If the sheet of a square sail carries away, the sail should be clewed up immediately to prevent it from ripping itself to shreds. It is impossible to clew down the upper three yards since the clewline on the affected side does not have any effect in pulling the yard down. Nevertheless, clewing up causes most of the wind to be spilled from the sails. The yards should come down by their own weight.

b. If the sheet of the headsail or staysail carries away, the sail should be blanketed by falling off and should be doused as quickly as possible. In the case of the mizzen staysails, where the whipping sheet pendant and block may endanger personnel, the halyard should be thrown off even before the downhaul is manned. The force of the wind along the leech should douse the sail.

c. If the *downhaul of a headsail or staysail* parts, the ship should fall off. The force of the wind on the leech should be enough to force the sail down or cadets may be stationed at the tack to pull it down by hand. If the sail jams, a line should be looped around the stay above the sail to pull it down.

d. If a weather *brace* should carry away, the yard will fly up against the lee backstays, imposing a dangerous strain on them. The ship should fall off so that the strain is taken by the other brace. The clewlines above and below the yard whose brace has carried away should be set taut to help control the yard. In marginal conditions where the ship is rolling, it may be beneficial to lash the yard against the shrouds until a new brace can be rove.

e. If the *spanker sheet* carries away, the boom will slam violently against the backstays. The preventer should be hauled taut to control the boom and the sail brailed in as soon as possible. If the boom cannot be controlled by the preventer, it should be lashed to the stays until a new sheet can be rove.

f. If the *fore* or *main yard lift* carries away, the shift of weight of the course yard may tear the lower topsail or the course, or part the sheets or tacks. If the sheets or tacks are intact, a strain can be taken on the clewlines and clewgarnets to keep the yard from working up and down. If the sheets or tacks have carried away, the course and lower topsail should be doused and the yard lashed to the backstays until the lifts can be replaced.

2. Standing rigging and gear carried away:

a. If the *bobstay* or any *forward leading stay* parts, the ship should fall off to remove all strain. Sail should be reduced if the ship is laboring. A jury stay should be rigged. In the case of the bobstay, a chain can be passed from the end of the bowsprit through the hawspipes and set taut with the capstan.

b. If a *backstay* or *shroud* parts, the ship should be wore immediately to place the strain on the opposite stay. Speed is of the essence here because the remaining stays will have to make up for the support of the damaged stay and a chain reaction might occur. After coming about, a new stay or preventer can be rigged.

c. If a *truss* or *shoe* carries away, the yard should be braced aback and lashed in place. The sails bent and sheeted to it should be doused before making repairs.

d. If a *spar* carries away, the lines attached to the spar, such as the sheets, clewlines, braces, and halyards should be handled in such a way as to minimize the motion of the yard in order to keep it from causing more damage. The spar should also be temporarily lashed in place to prevent its causing more damage or crashing to the deck while gear is rigged to lower it to deck. If a spar carries over the side, it should be recovered if possible. If it endangers the hull, however, it should be cut away immediately.

e. If there is a *steering casualty* caused by a failure in the linkage between the helm and the rudder, control should be shifted to after steering. The *trick wheel* is engaged by aligning its gears with those of the rudder gearing and by pulling the control handle all the way forward to engage the gears. Sound-powered telephone talkers should be assigned to relay courses from the bridge. After the casualty has been repaired, it will be necessary to set both the rudder and *helm indicator* amidships and to line up the gears of the rudder mechanism with those of the main helm before pulling the control handle all the way aft to engage the gears.

SHIP EMERGENCIES

Man Overboard

The virtue of forehandedness in a good seaman is absolutely necessary for the safe recovery of a man overboard. The watch officer must continually reevaluate winds and seas throughout his watch since his actions for recovering a man overboard vary with the conditions. It is equally important that he ensure that his watch is briefed and ready for any eventuality. In particular, the Ready Boat Crew must be properly organized in order to lower away expeditiously.

Any person seeing a crew member go over the side must sing out *"Man overboard port (starboard) side"* and must ensure that his report reaches the bridge. As many life rings as possible are thrown to the person. Ships in company are notified by radio and by use of the *Oscar* flag or man overboard lights (rapidly flashing not-under-command lights). Five or more blasts are sounded to alert other ships and the crew of the emergency.

In CIC, the dead reckoning tracer (DRT) should be set to the 200 yard/inch scale and the initial position of the person marked. The estimated bearing and range of the person should be reported every fifteen seconds. If the person is in sight, the watch officer should take visual bearings and pass them back to CIC so that they may update their plot.

The height of eye on the bridge of the *Eagle* is so low that the person will be quickly lost unless kept constantly in sight. The OOD must not let any other detail detract from his keeping the person in sight. This is particularly important when under sail because the bearing of the person normally drifts forward as the ship comes up into the wind, remains steady as the ship loses way, and then moves aft as the ship falls off. The signal watch and other cadets should lay to the tops as soon as possible and point to the person with outstretched arms. Similarly, any personnel on deck not otherwise engaged should point at the person to help the OOD in case he loses sight of the person.

The way in which the ship should be maneuvered to recover the person depends on wind and sea conditions and on whether the ship is sailing or under power (figure 44).

1. If *under sail,* the ship should be brought up into the wind always except when the weather is so severe that the ship itself may be endangered. After giving the helm command to bring the ship up, the OOD should concentrate on lowering the

boat and keeping the person in sight. The sails will take care of themselves until the full crew arrives on deck, at which time the sailing master or another officer can take charge of sail evolutions. When sufficient personnel have arrived on deck to handle sail, the ship should be brought to.

a. When *on the wind,* it is desirable to tack so that when the ship lies to, it will slowly drift down in the direction of the person in the water. In this case, *"Mainsail haul"* should be ordered, as in tacking. As the ship passes through the wind, however, *"Let go and haul"* is not given in order that the ship lies to with the foretopsail to the mast. The mainsails will draw while the foresails will back, and the ship will come dead in the water or will have only slight headway. If the ship does not make it through the wind, no harm is done because the ship will lie with the main topsail to the mast, with the fore drawing and the main backing. After the yards have been braced, the sails can then be doused or trimmed as necessary.

In coming up into the wind, the OOD must carefully judge conditions so that the proper boat may be lowered. If the original lee boat is dropped, it will have to be picked up on the weather side if the ship goes through the wind—a dangerous operation. Thus, he must lower the boat that will be in the lee when the ship lies to.

b. When *off the wind* there is little possibility that ship will make it through the wind; thus, the main objective is to stop the ship as quickly as possible. In this case it is best to let go and haul in order to box off the fore. The fore will back more effectively

Figure 44. Man overboard procedures under sail and power.

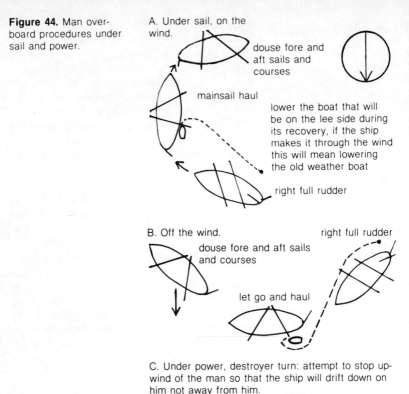

A. Under sail, on the wind.

douse fore and aft sails and courses

mainsail haul

lower the boat that will be on the lee side during its recovery, if the ship makes it through the wind this will mean lowering the old weather boat

right full rudder

B. Off the wind.

right full rudder

douse fore and aft sails and courses

let go and haul

C. Under power, destroyer turn: attempt to stop upwind of the man so that the ship will drift down on him not away from him.

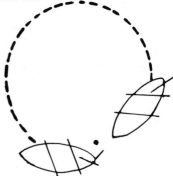

D. Under power, modified destroyer turn: stay on original course until the man is well astern before commencing the turn. This will allow a straight in final approach and will ensure that the ship can be maneuvered upwind of the man.

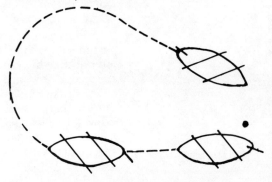

E. Under power, Williamson turn: used for low visibility or night situations. This maneuver returns the ship to the reciprocal of its track line.

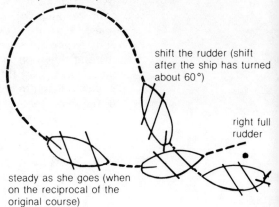

shift the rudder (shift after the ship has turned about 60°)

right full rudder

steady as she goes (when on the reciprocal of the original course)

G. Maneuvers when motor-sailing depend on the wind and sea conditions and the sails set. Usually the ship will maneuver as if under power alone unless strong winds would prevent the ship from turning.

than the main, which is blanketed by the fore as the ship comes up into the wind. After bracing, the fore-and-aft sails and courses may be doused at leisure. The ship will lie to with the foresails backing and the mainsails drawing.

In either case, sail handling is done by personnel arriving on deck. The watch, after putting the rudder over, is completely engaged in lowering away and actually recovering the person.

2. If *under power*, the engine is used to bring the ship back to the vicinity of the person. The approach depends on wind and sea conditions and whether any sails are set.

a. If under *engine alone*, a ship pickup may be attempted. The rudder should be put over full on the side where the person went over in order to swing the stern away. In calm weather, a *destroyer turn* should be made. This involves coming around a full 360°, stopping upwind of the person, and drifting down on him. Due to the tremendous windage of the *Eagle*'s tophamper, it will be difficult to complete the turn upwind of the person if there is much wind. A boat must be lowered when the ship nears the person.

Because of the difficulty with the destroyer turn in stopping upwind of the person, a modified turn may be preferable when a good breeze is blowing. For this method, the ship remains on its initial course until the person is about one hundred yards astern, and is then brought around full. The extra distance before turning allows a straight approach as the ship comes about and heads toward the person; it also makes it much easier to stop upwind of the person.

In low visibility or at night, the *Williamson turn* is preferred. The rudder is put over full in the direction of the person, but is shifted once the ship has swung 60°. In this way the ship will return to a reciprocal of its original track.

b. If *motor sailing,* a careful judgment of circumstances must be made. In very light winds or with only fore-and-aft sails, it may be possible to make a ship pickup by using the engines to force the ship through the wind. In moderate winds it will probably be necessary to handle sail much as if the ship were under sail alone. If on the wind, they should be handled as in tacking, using the engine to make sure the ship passes through the wind. If off the wind, it may be best to use the engine to force a wear by falling off rather than merely backing the fore to lie to. The actual method used in motor sailing depends on the conditions of wind, sea, and sail when the person goes overboard.

Collision Imminent

So few square-rigged vessels remain afloat that meeting one at sea is something of a rarity. Unfortunately, many ships, upon sighting the *Eagle,* will come in close to take a look. At night many often fail to recognize her red-over-green sailing lights (which cannot be seen as far as a motor vessel's white lights); thus, they fail to recognize her right of way in crossing situations. When she is under sail, the maneuvering options open to the *Eagle* are quite limited compared to those of a motor vessel. Early action, therefore, is particularly important in avoiding close quarters situations.

As on any cutter, a careful radar plot and record of visual bearings should be maintained. As soon as it becomes evident that a close quarters situation is developing, communication with the inbound vessel should be attempted by VHF-FM radio on Channel 16 offshore and Channel 13 in U.S. coastal waters. As the ship continues in, communication should be attempted by flashing light and the danger signal sounded on the whistle when appropriate. Since it takes at least fifteen minutes to put the engine on the line even in an emergency situation, an early decision must be made whether to order it up. At night, if the previous action is unsuccessful, the sails should be illuminated by means of the working floodlights.

If a collision becomes imminent, the *collision alarm* must be sounded and the highest state of material readiness (*Zebra*) set. How the ship is to be maneuvered depends on wind and sea conditions and on the relative size and maneuverability of the two vessels. In general, however, the ship should be turned to reduce the relative motion between the two ships as much as possible so that a *sideswipe,* rather than a head-on collision, occurs. The large size of the *Eagle*'s compartments and the limited number of watertight bulkheads and the fact that the majority of the crew berth in the midships area of the ship make it particularly important that the *Eagle* not be hit broadside. Thus, it may be preferable to turn in to the incoming vessel and present the bows. The bowsprit will absorb much of the force of a collision and, hopefully, will limit most of the damage to areas above the waterline.

In deciding on action to avoid collision, the OOD must carefully evaluate the probable actions of the watch-officer on the other vessel after the latter realizes that a collision situation has developed. As required by both the Inland and International Rules of the Road, the "give way" (burdened) vessel must, if possible, avoid crossing ahead of the "stand on" (privileged) vessel. In particular, Rule 17c of the International Rules of the Road specifically forbids the "stand on" vessel from altering course to port for a vessel on her own port side "if the circumstances of the case admit." Nevertheless, Rule 17b does allow "such action as will best aid to avoid collision" once the vessels are so close that action by the "give way" vessel would not be sufficient of itself to prevent collision (*in extremis*). Thus, in all cases the action by the *Eagle*'s OOD must be consistent with the most probable avoidance maneuvers of the other vessel and, as far as possible, the Rules of the Road should be strictly followed.

No one likes to think of collision, but forehanded evaluation of the possibilities can minimize the damage. Obviously, if at all possible, collision should be avoided. Early action, then, is required before close quarters are reached.

8. Eagle Seamanship

Equipment

With minor exceptions in the locations of such things as cleats, bitts, padeyes, winches, and stowage of falls, the boat davits and associated equipment on the *Eagle* are representative of boat handling gear in any ship. The procedures and commands used aboard the *Eagle* will also apply, with some modifications, to any ship. The following gear is used in boat operations.

Boat davits are of the quadrantal type. They are capable of carrying the boats rigged in or rigged out for sea.

Boat falls of 4″, three-strand, right-laid manila line are reeved in a two-fold purchase. The falls are belayed to a fitting on the davits called a crucifix. When not in use, the falls are neatly arranged on the davit screw sheath covers. Prior to lowering, the falls are faked out on deck so that they are free for running.

The *lower block* of the falls is a non-toppling, double-sheaved block. An oval-shaped eye on the bottom of the lower block engages a spring-loaded safety hook on the Rottimer release gear in the boat. The *Rottimer release gear* is used to attach the boat to the falls. The spring-loaded hook in the boat, which attaches to the oval eye of the block, is normally held in the upright position by a slotted collar that may be rotated 180° with a handle. The handle is held in the closed position with a lanyard. When the boat is lowered and the command *"Unhook"* is given, the lanyard is removed from the lever, the lever is swung 180° to the open position, and the hook topples, releasing the eye of the block.

As soon as the falls are unhooked, the block is passed over the gunwales, the hook is placed back in the collar, and the handle is rotated to the closed position and secured by a lanyard.

When hooking up, the eye of the block is swung smoothly past the spring-loaded keepers of the safety latch. The block must be held in an upright position while the slack is taken out of the falls. The hook men must continue to hold on to the handles on the cheeks of the block, keeping them upright until the boat is clear of the water. Hook men must be prepared to rotate the blocks to take any turns out of the falls.

The *frapping line* is simple in design and purpose. It is tended on deck and controls the swing of the falls as the boat is raised and lowered. The falls are reeved through a ring called a traveling lizard, at the end of the frapping line.

The *sea painter* is a line of such length that when the boat is riding the sea painter alongside the ship, the boat is positioned under the falls, thus facilitating the *hooking on* evolution. One end of the sea painter is secured to a cleat near the bow of the boat, the other end to a bitt in the forward part of the waist of the ship. When rigged, the sea painter is led *under* the frapping line and the mainsail sheet.

Deck Detail

The lowering and recovery detail consists of the following personnel:

a. The *boatswain's mate* [BM] is in charge of lowering and hoisting the boat. The BM is responsible for the overall supervision and safety of the operation. He or she must use standard commands and must give them in a loud clear voice so that those who must act on the commands can hear them.

b. *Falls tenders.* There are two cadets on each fall. One actually controls the falls and the other backs that person up. When lowering the boat, the falls tenders keep their eyes on the crucifix, glance at the falls, and listen to the BM. The falls are smoothly eased *hand over hand* but hands *must* be kept a forearm's distance away *from* the crucifix. When hoisting, the tenders watch the falls on the drum of the winch, and listen to the BM.

c. *Frapping line tenders.* There is one cadet on each frapping line. Their job is to eliminate as much transverse swing of the falls and boat as possible.

d. *Fender men:* Two cadets who keep fenders between the ship and the boat.

e. *Sea painter tenders:* One cadet who retrieves the sea painter and coils it in preparation for passing when the boat returns and one additional cadet who assists and is ready with a stand-by heaving line. There should *not* be less than two heaving lines available for use at this location.

f. *Winch operator:* The individual who operates the winch as directed by the BM.

g. *Stopper men:* Two cadets who pass the stoppers when ordered.

Boat Crew

The following are the minimum personnel assignments for a boat crew:

a. The *coxswain* is in charge of preparing the boat for launching and is also in charge of the boat as soon as it is waterborne. He ensures that the boat crew is in proper uniform and equipped with life jackets (all ties and straps properly secured) and exposure suits, if appropriate. At night, life jacket lights must be on.

The coxswain is responsible for ensuring that the boat crew is thoroughly familiar with its duties and is briefed prior to laying into the boat. He should question the boat engineer as to the status of the engine, water, lube oil, and fuel. Except when unavoidable, a boat should never depart with less than a full tank of fuel.

Finally, the coxswain should ensure that the boat is equipped with operating VHF-FM radio and that a satisfactory communications check is made *before lowering*.

b. The *boat engineer* is responsible to the coxswain for the proper operation of the boat engine and for quickly making the necessary checks prior to launching.

On the coxswain's order, prior to the boat becoming waterborne, the engineer starts the engine. When the boat is waterborne, he ensures that the engine has sea water suction and then reports this to the coxswain. The sea painter should not be cast off until the engine has sea water suction. While the boat is underway, the engineer makes checks of the engine to assure its continued proper operation.

NOTE: As most boat evolutions are carried out under emergency conditions, such as a man overboard, the boat will daily receive a thorough checkout. Thus, it requires only minimal checks prior to launching.

c. The *bow hook*, on command, unhooks and hooks forward, and tends the sea painter.

d. The *stern hook*, on command, unhooks and hooks aft.

Lowering the Boat

The procedure and commands for lowering the boat (assuming the boat is rigged out) are as follows:

a. Boatswain's mate: (After ensuring that all is in readiness on deck and that stations are properly manned) *"One man (designate) lay into the boat"*. This cadet removes lashings and makes whatever checks are necessary to ensure that the boat is ready for launching. He should be equipped with a life jacket, properly secured, before getting into the boat.

b. Boatswain's mate: *"Cast off the gripe"*. This is done by one of the frapping line tenders. The cadet in the boat passes the gripe inboard of the poop deck rail.

c. Boatswain's mate: *"Cast off the preventers"* (if rigged). The cadet in the boat trips the pelican hooks on the preventers.

d. Boatswain's mate: *"Boat crew lay into the boat"*. The crew lays into the boat and grasps man ropes. As the boat is lowered and raised, each person should support his own weight on the man rope.

e. Coxswain: When satisfied that all is ready in the boat, informs the BM: *"Ready in the boat"*.

f. Boatswain's mate: Reports to the OOD: *"Ready on deck"*.

g. Boatswain's mate: When he receives permission from the OOD, commands *"On the falls. Take off all but one round turn and half a figure eight"*.

h. Boatswain's mate: Inquires *"Ready forward/aft?"*

i. Boatswain's mate: Upon confirmation that both falls are ready, commands *"Lower away together"*, then *"Lively/Easy forward/aft"* as appropriate.

j. Boatswain's mate: As the ship rolls toward the side from which the boat is lowered, and the boat is lifted on a swell, commands *"Let fall"*. At this point the coxswain is in charge.

k. Coxswain: Commands *"Unhook aft."* After receiving the report and visually confirming that the after falls are unhooked, commands *"Unhook forward"*.
NOTE: The after falls must be unhooked before the forward falls.

1. Coxswain: When the falls are clear he shears the boat out riding on the sea painter, and when permission is received from the bridge, commands *"Cast off the sea painter"*. (Do not cast off the sea painter until the engine has sea water suction and a catenary has developed in the sea painter.)

Raising the Boat

The procedures and commands for raising the boat are as follows:

a. Boatswain's mate to OOD: *"Ready on deck,"* when rigged to pick up the boat and all personnel are at their assigned stations.

b. Bridge/OOD: *"Come alongside and receive the sea painter"*.

c. Bridge/OOD: When the boat is paralleling the course of the ship (about 25 ft. away and opposite the position of the cadet who will pass the painter) in position to receive the sea painter, commands *"Pass the sea painter"*. The cadet on deck passes a heaving line to which the sea painter is secured. The bow hook makes the sea painter fast to the bow cleat of the boat, utilizing the toggle, and the coxswain then rides the sea painter.

d. Bridge/OOD: *"Lay under the falls and hook on"*.

e. Coxswain: When under the davits with the falls in position commands *"Hook on forward."* When hooked on forward, commands *"Hook on aft"*.

f. Coxswain: When all is ready in the boat, reports *"Ready in the boat"*.

NOTE: At this point the boatswain's mate is again in charge.

g. Boatswain's mate: *"Heave around together."* The winch man moves his control lever to slow, then immediately to high, speed.

The commands "Lively" and "Easy" are not used when hoisting with a winch. To even up the boat, it is necessary to go slower on one fall and the command *"Surge forward/aft"* is given by the BM. To comply, the falls tender allows the five turns on the appropriate drum of the winch to slip slightly, i.e., surge. When the boat is on an even keel, *"Heave around together"* is again given.

h. Boatswain's mate: When the boat is at the rail, commands *"Avast heaving"*. The winch man moves his control to stop and the falls are held on the drum.

i. Boatswain's mate: *"Boat crew lay out of the boat"*.

j. Boatswain's mate: When the crew is out of the boat, commands *"Pass stoppers fore and aft"*.

k. Boatswain's mate: When informed "Stoppers passed fore/aft," commands *"Forward, back easy."* The strain is then transferred from the winch drum to the passed stopper. If the stopper holds, it is reported to the BM by the man passing the stopper ("Stopper holding forward"). The BM commands *"Forward, up behind"*. The forward falls are belayed to the crucifix.

Should the stopper not hold, the BM will command *"Set taut"* and the strain will again be taken by the winch until the stopper is passed again.

When the falls are secured forward, the BM commands *"Aft, back easy"* and the process is repeated for the after falls.

After the falls have been belayed, the boat davits are cranked in, the gripe is passed and made up securely, all gear is restowed, and lines are made up.

Safety Notes

Each member of the boat crew, and anyone going into the boat for any reason, must wear a life jacket.

Man ropes are provided for the safety of the boat crew. They must be used whenever the boat is not completely rigged for sea, i.e., when raising or lowering, and when alongside but not secured. Personnel in the boat during lowering or raising operations must use the man rope to support their own weight.

The most critical phase of raising and lowering operations is the transition between the time the boat is fully waterborne and the time that it is clear of the water. During this time, the boat and falls are under the greatest stress due to the working of the ship in the sea way. This period must be made as short as possible by rapid raising or lowering.

All personnel involved should remain alert, pay attention to their immediate job, and keep silent unless required to speak.

The boat crew must keep their hands inside the boat and off the gunwales.

Ground Tackle

Anchors aboard the *Eagle* include:

2 Patent (Dumm) 3500 lbs., port:
Navy Patent anchor
3800 lbs., stbd:
Original German
anchor

Chain on board consists of:

Starboard chain	135	fathoms
		(9 shots)
Connecting shot	3.5	fathoms
Swivel shot	1.7	fathoms
Total length	140.2	fathoms

Port chain	135	fathoms
		(9 shots)
Connecting shot	3.5	fathoms
Swivel shot	1.7	fathoms
Total length	140.2	fathoms

Both chains are 1.75'' wire diameter.

The chains are marked according to the normal Coast Guard system in 15-fathom shots. The first shot is measured from the jew's harp and includes the bending and swivel shots.

Ground Tackle Operation

The anchor handling machinery on the *Eagle* consists of an electrically driven capstan coupled through a clutch to the wildcats (drums with sprockets which hold the links of the anchor chain as it is raised or lowered). The gears and shafting between the capstan are below the deck. Aft and inboard of each wildcat is a two-position lever which engages it to the capstan. On top of each wildcat is a hand-wheel clutch control. It is used to disengage the wildcat so that it will run freely when the anchor is let go and to engage it when the anchor is to be heaved up. When the anchor is let go, the chain is controlled by a band-type brake controlled by a hand-wheel abaft each wildcat.

Prior to 1954, the anchor was weighed by hand in the traditional manner by turning the capstan with capstan bars. Although the electric capstan is normally used now, it is still possible to disengage the electric motor and it is still possible to operate the capstan by hand.

Chain stoppers consisting of several chain links, a turnbuckle, and a pelican hook are provided for each chain. These chain stoppers are shackled to the deck and attached to the chain forward of the wildcat. They are used to secure the anchor for sea, for holding it when it is made ready for letting go, and to hold the anchor in the hawse in case the need arises to unshackle the chain from the anchor. Immediately forward of the chain stoppers are two chain pawls. These are safety devices that would come into use should a chain stopper or the brake fail. The capstan is equipped with pawls. These are what a landsman might call ratchets. They were of considerable importance when the capstan was hand-powered, for they ensured that the capstan could not be operated inadvertently in the wrong direction. Now that the capstan is normally operated by power and can be operated in both directions, it is necessary to ensure that the pawls are in the *up* position.

When word is passed to prepare to bring the ship to anchor, the first lieutenant, who is in charge on the forecastle, musters his anchor detail. He ascertains whether the port or starboard or both anchors are to be used. If not done previously, he requests that the engine room provide power to the anchor windlass. The quarter-deck should have notified the engine room previously of the time of anchoring. Both anchors always are made ready for letting go. In addition, the first lieutenant receives any special instructions and is advised as to the depth of the water and type of bottom.

It is very rare that a person has a reason to be in the chain locker. However, it is mandatory that the first lieutenant ascertain that no person is in the chain locker. It is also wise to inspect the chain in the bin to ensure that no foreign objects are fouled in it.

If anchor buoys are used, the buoy of the appropriate green or red color is bent to the anchor. Sufficient scope is used on the buoy line to ensure that it will float. However, the line is short enough to ensure that it will float almost directly over the anchor.

The capstan is then engaged to the wildcat of the anchor which is being prepared for letting go. A light strain is taken on the chain. At the same time, the brake is backed off. An additional strain is taken on the chain, if necessary, until it is possible to raise the chain pawl. The brake is then set up taut and the capstan stopped. The pelican hook of the chain stopper is moved back two links and reattached. The direction of the capstan is reversed, the brake eased, and the chain walked out (or eased out slowly, link by link) until the strain is taken by the stopper and there is slack between the chain stopper and the wildcat. The capstan is stopped, the brake is again set taut, and the clutch of the wildcat is disengaged. The two links of chain have been backed out so that it is known that the anchor is not jammed in the hawse and so that the entire strain of the anchor is taken by the chain stopper. With the strain on the stopper, the anchor can be let go by tripping the pelican hook of the stopper. No other controls need be adjusted.

It may be that the anchor has been ordered walked out to the water's edge or, when anchoring in deep water, even further. The same process is used except that, of course, the distance is greater than two links.

Letting Go

When the ship nears the desired anchorage point, the word is passed from the quarterdeck to *"Stand by the starboard (port) anchor."* The first lieutenant orders the brake released, orders all hands abaft the wildcats, and orders the pin removed from the retaining bail of the pelican hook on the appropriate chain stopper. At this point, the first lieutenant is normally advised as to the desired scope of chain and whether this will be measured *"on deck"* or *"at the water's edge."* This scope is an integral number of shots and is expressed as *"One shot on deck"* or *"Three shots at the water's edge."*

When the ship comes to the desired spot, the command is given from the quarterdeck to *"Let go the starboard (port) anchor."* This command must be executed without delay. The retaining bail of the pelican hook on the chain stopper is knocked clear with a maul and the anchor is run clear. The damage controlman, whose duty it is to tend the brake, allows the anchor to run freely until it touches the bottom, at which time he sets up a few turns on the brake to prevent the chain from overhauling itself and piling up on the bottom. Since the chain runs rapidly and often throws off rust chips, the damage controlman and other personnel in the immediate area must wear protective masks or goggles. If the ship has been properly handled, she has a slight amount of sternway, or perhaps headway, if brought to anchor under sail. The chain is allowed to run out to the desired scope, at which time the brake is set taut. If the ship were not moving, the anchor chain would pile up on the bottom and might foul the anchor. During this time, the first lieutenant makes reports to the quarter-deck relative to the direction the chain is tending, using the "clock" system (12 o'clock being dead ahead), and the amount of strain on the chain. When a good strain is on the chain and the chain goes slack, the first lieutenant is satisfied that the anchor has taken a good bite in the bottom. He reports *"Anchor brought to and holding."* Unless it is desirable to add to the scope (veer chain) or shorten the scope, the anchor detail is normally told to secure it. The chain stopper is passed. The brake is backed off so that the strain may come on the chain stopper, and the chain between the wildcat and the stopper goes slack. The brake is then set taut and the pawl dropped. No strain comes on the pawl, for it is merely a safety device to be used if the chain stopper fails. If some of the strain is allowed to come on the pawl and it becomes desirable to veer chain, it could not be accomplished until the chain is heaved in to release the strain and raise the pawl.

Weighing Anchor

Prior to weighing anchor, the engine room is notified so that sufficient electrical power is available to operate the capstan and so that there is sufficient pressure on the fire main to wash the chain and anchor as they are heaved in.

When the anchor detail is set (before heaving in and weighing anchor), the first lieutenant must check the following details: that sufficient personnel are available; that the vertical shaft to the electrical motor is engaged; that the selector clutch is engaged to connect the capstan to the wildcat; that the wildcat clutch is engaged; that one or more fire hoses are rigged to wash the anchor and chain as they are heaved in; and that no person or foreign object is in the chain locker.

When all of these things have been done, the first lieutenant reports "*Ready to heave around.*" When the order to *heave around* is given, the capstan is started and the brake is backed off a few turns. When the chain stopper goes slack, it is knocked clear and the brake backed off all the way. The pawl remains down and rides over each link as it is heaved in. This is a safety feature to be used if something should happen to the wildcat. As the anchor is being heaved in, the first lieutenant makes reports relative to the direction the anchor is tending and the amount of strain on the chain. When the anchor comes to short stay (when all slack chain has been heaved in and the shank of the anchor is just about to be lifted from the bottom), the first lieutenant orders *"Avast heaving"* and reports *"Anchor at short stay."* Should there occur a delay in any of the other preparations for getting underway, there will still be time as the vessel will be (barely) anchored. When all is in readiness, the first lieutenant is ordered to *"Break out the anchor."* Heaving in is resumed. When the chain is nearly straight up and down and a considerable strain comes on the anchor windlass, the anchor is reported as *"Up and down."* As soon as the anchor breaks out, the anchor windlass speeds up and the report *"Anchor's aweigh"* is made.

Next comes the order *"House the anchor."* The anchor is heaved all the way in, the brake set taut, and the capstan stopped. Great care must be exercised here, as a severe strain can come on the anchor windlass. If allowed to continue for more than a second, it can do great damage. When the brake has been set taut, the chain stopper is passed. Unless orders to the contrary are received, the anchor is again made ready for letting go and remains ready until the special sea detail and the anchor detail are secured. When they are secured, the anchors are made ready for sea and the engine room advised that the capstan is secured.

If, when the anchor approaches the hawse pipe, both flukes are pointed inboard, they slide up the side in that position and press on the skin of the ship as the shank starts to enter the hawse, threatening to puncture the side and preventing the anchor from being fully housed. To *trip the flukes* so they point outboard, a bight of line is lowered over the anchor and is brought up snug under the flukes and each end is secured on deck. The anchor is then backed out. As it is lowered, the line keeps the flukes up, tending to pivot them. Finally, they flop over and point outboard. With the flukes tripped into their normal position, the line is brought back aboard and the anchor housed as described above.

RIGGING GEAR ALOFT

Bending a Square Sail

The sail is stretched along the deck, after side down, and the head is stretched well out. The sail is then gathered up as in furling and gaskets are passed snugly around it, leaving the tabling at the head and foot clear. The leech cringles, for sails with leechlines or bunt-leechlines are also exposed.

A gantline is then passed around the center of the sail and is swayed aloft to the yard where it is bent. It is hoisted far enough above the yard so that the men on the yard can grasp it by the head cringles and fleet it out along the yardarms as the gantline is eased off. As soon as possible, the head earring is taken through its eye on the end of the yard and brought back through the head cringle. This then serves as a tackle to help extend the head of the sail. The sail is hauled well out with the head earrings as the gantline is further slacked away, until the special hooks on the earring jackstays at the end of the yardarms can be passed through the head cringles. The sail is then carefully centered on the yard and the center roband is passed and secured. An additional turn is taken with the head ear-ring or, in the case of the lower sails, a jig-ger is hooked in to the head cringles. The tabling along the head of the sail is stretched taut, after which the head ear-rings are secured and remaining robands are passed around the jackstays. Sheets, clewlines, leechlines, bunt-leechlines, and buntlines are bent to the sail; it is then ready for setting. In bending the gear, con-siderable care and foresight is necessary to avoid turns and to ensure that everything will run fair when the sail is set. If the sail is first set in blowing weather, any fouled gear may result in serious trouble. If the sail is being bent in harbor, it is let fall and then furled with the gear to ensure that every-thing is properly led and bent.

**Bending a
Fore-and-Aft Sail**

A fore-and-aft sail is made up along the foot and swayed out or up to the stay upon which it is to be bent. The halyard and downhaul are bent into the head cringle, and the tack is made fast to ensure that the sail will not be lost. The luff of the sail is then bent to the hanks on the stay, starting at the head and working down. In harbor or in fair weather, this may be accomplished most easily by running the sail partly up the stay as the robands are passed on the indi-vidual hanks. The sheets are shackled to the clew cringle and the sail is ready to go to work.

**Housing and Unhousing
the Topgallant Mast**

The *Eagle* was designed to be able to transit the Kiel Canal in Germany, where the vertical clearance is approximately 135 feet. Since the mast height of the fore and main is 147 feet (originally 150.3 feet), the topgallant mast was designed to be lowered by about 15 feet. The process requires the topgallant yard to be first unshipped and secured in a special *winter housing,* a fitting on the forward part of the topmast cap band. The topgallant mast is then lowered by means of the upper topsail halyard which has been rigged to a mast rope.

The procedure for stepping and unstepping the mast is complicated and requires trained personnel. It is normally done only by the enlisted deck force. As a result, the following description is designed for persons already expert in seamanship rather than for cadets. With a trained crew and good conditions, both masts may be unstepped in under five hours.

Preparation

The mast rope, which consists of 100 feet of ⁵/₉″ wire with a soft eye in the upper end and a teardrop thimble in the lower end, must first be rigged. The soft eye enables the wire to be reeved through the athwartship sheave in the base of the topgallant mast. The mast rope is reeved through a block shackled to a padeye on the topmast cap band, and down through the sheave in the topgallant mast base. It is then shackled to the padeye on the topmast cap band opposite that to which the block is shackled. Before shackling it to the topmast cap band, a teardrop thimble should be seized into the soft eye to keep from damaging the wire.

After the mast rope has been rigged, the rigging must be slacked. The royal and topgallant backstays should be slacked at least eight turns, the royal and topgallant stays on the main at least six turns, and the royal and flying jib stays on the fore at least eight turns. The topgallant shrouds are slacked after the topgallant yard is unshipped.

Unshipping the Topgallant Yard

The topgallant yard must be unshipped in order to clear the lower part of the topgallant mast for lowering. The following gear is required: a 1½-ton come-along, 5 fathoms of 6 thread, a marlin spike, two nylon straps, and a Chicago Grip.

The topgallant sheets and clewlines should be thrown off and the horizontal position of the yard controlled by the royal sheets. The topgallant halyard should be heaved until the yard is high enough to disconnect the lifts from the mast (not from the yard arms).

After the lifts have been removed, the halyard should be eased until the yard reaches the lower portion of the topgallant track; it should not be set on the stop bolt at the lower end of the track. After the halyard has been belayed, the bight of a nylon strap should be placed forward of the topgallant halyard tye pad on the yard and the ends of the strap should be led down around the aft side of the yard and back up the forward side. The control end of the come-along should be hooked onto this strap and the other end hooked on the flying jib stay on the fore or the topgallant stay on the main. When it is rigged, the come-along should be jacked until a neutral position, where the weight of the yard is held by the halyard and come-along rather than by the truss pin in the shoe, is reached. When this occurs, the pin should be removed and the yard eased forward until it is clear of the shoe.

When the yard is clear, the halyard and

come-along should be eased until the yard is forward of its winter socket on the topmast cap band. It should then be eased into the fitting and the pin inserted. The halyard can then be removed from the topgallant yard by hooking the come-along into the tye padeye on the yard and extending it to its full length. The Chicago Grip should be placed on the halyard and the extended end of the come-along hooked in. The come-along is then jacked until the topgallant fly block is pulled up to a position just aft of the cross-tree spreaders where it can be secured. Once secure, the tye can be disconnected from the topgallant yard and eased up through the cloak block, and then down to the cross-trees where it can be coiled and seized. The mast is now ready for housing.

Housing the Mast

While the topgallant yard is being unshipped, the men on deck should switch the upper topsail halyard purchase to the mast rope. The upper topsail tye chain should be lashed away from the top of the upper topsail track to allow the topgallant mast to be lowered without jamming. The topgallant shrouds, halyards, and all other rigging to the topgallant mast should now be slacked and the mast rope (that is, the upper topsail halyard purchase) led to the waist deck winch. The rope should be heaved until the mast is raised approximately one inch so that the mast *fid*, which supports the mast when shipped, may be removed.

After the fid has been removed, the mast should be eased down until about 3 feet of topgallant track is left above the topmast cap. The stop bolt at the head of the topgallant track should be removed, the yard shoe slid up and off the track, and the bolt replaced. The wedges are then removed and the mast eased downward until the cloak block reaches the topmast cap. A bar of 1″ round stock steel is placed into the top of the cloak block. The mast is eased down until the bar lays across the topmast cap aft and the band forward, supporting the weight of the mast. The mast is unshipped and all gear may be made up.

Stepping the Mast

Stepping the topgallant mast is essentially the reciprocal of housing it. Any tightened gear leading to the topgallant mast is again slacked. The mast rope is led to the deck winch and is heaved around until the mast rope bears the entire weight of the mast. The bar is then removed from the topgallant cloak block and the mast is raised until about 3 feet of the topgallant track show above the topmast band. The stop bolt at the head of the track is removed, the yard shoe put on, and the bolt replaced. The mast is then raised until the mast fid can be replaced, at which time the mast wedges are set and the topgallant shrouds tightened evenly. Finally, all other stays and backstays can be tightened easily as long as they are clear of the topgallant yard.

Shipping the Topgallant Yard

While the stays are being tightened, the upper topsail tye chain can be shifted to the front side of the mast. The topgallant tye should then be led up through the cloak block and back down to the yard where it is shackled into the tye padeye. The gantline should be bent into the topgallant fly block with a bowline. The bight of the bowline should be about 5 feet long so that the knot can be cast off after the flyblock is eased down to its normal position.

When the gantline is rigged, a strain is taken until the strap holding the flyblock to the cross-trees is disconnected. It is then eased until the flyblock drops down to its normal position. The gantline is cast off and the topgallant halyards heaved handsomely until the gantline takes the weight of the yard. A strap is then rigged on the yard, as in unshipping, and the come-along rigged into the flying jib or topgallant stay (as appropriate) with the control end at the strap. The come-along is jacked until it supports some of the yard's weight. The topgallant sheets and clewlines are cast off and the yard's horizontal position is controlled by the royal sheets. When all is ready, the pin is pulled from the winter housing.

The come-along is heaved until the yard is clear of the housing. Then, the topgallant halyard is heaved until the yard is up to the shoe on the track. The come-along is used to hold the yard away from the mast as it goes up. The yard is then eased into the shoe by carefully adjusting the come-along and halyard. Once the pin has been replaced in the shoe, the come-along is removed and the yard is heaved up until the lifts may be reinstalled.

Dressing and Full-Dressing Ship

The ship is dressed or full-dressed on national holidays and for special ceremonies. The procedures for dressing and full-dressing are prescribed by *Coast Guard Regulations* (CG-300) and the Navy publication *Flags and Pennants* (DNC-27). The

Figure 45.

blocks placed on fore and after sides of mast to handle hoist

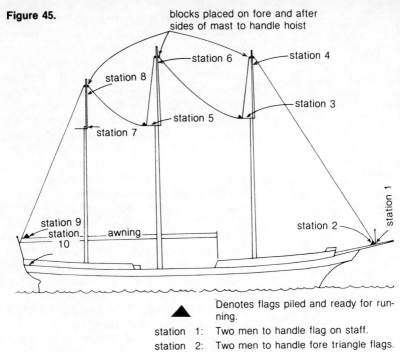

▲ Denotes flags piled and ready for running.

station 1: Two men to handle flag on staff.

station 2: Two men to handle fore triangle flags.

station 3: Two men to tend halyards, one man to handle fore-to-main flags.

station 4: One man to place blocks and observe hoist, handles fouls and other emergencies at blocks.

station 5: Two men to tend halyards; one man to handle main-to-mizzen flags.

station 6: One man to place blocks and observe hoist: handles fouls and other emergencies at blocks.

station 7: Three men to tend halyards and handle flags as required.

station 8: One man to place blocks and observe hoist; handles fouls and other emergencies at blocks.

station 9: One man to tend mizzen-to-stern flags.

station 10: Two men to handle flag on staff.

following procedures are used aboard the *Eagle:*

DRESSING SHIP

1. The largest National Ensign, with which the *Eagle* is furnished, is displayed at the flagstaff.

2. The Coast Guard Ensign is at the foretruck.

3. A National Ensign is flown at the maintruck.

4. One of the following flies at the mizzentruck: personal flag, command pennant, or commission pennant with a National Ensign.

5. When dressing or full-dressing the *Eagle* in honor of a foreign nation, the ensign of that nation replaces the United States National Ensign at the maintruck.

6. The *Eagle,* when not underway, is dressed or full-dressed from 0800 until sunset; when underway, she is never dressed or full-dressed.

7. When half-masting of the National Ensign is required on occasions of dressing or full-dressing ship, only the National Ensign at the flagstaff is half-masted.

FULL-DRESSING SHIP

1. On occasions of full-dressing ship, in addition to the dressing of the mastheads, a rainbow of signal flags, arranged in the order prescribed in *Flags and Pennants* (DNC-27) is displayed. It reaches from the foot of the jackstaff to the mastheads and then to the foot of the flagstaff.

1. 3-flag	4. SIERRA
2. 4-flag	5. 1st Sub.
3. 1-pennant	6. ALFA

7. PAPA	37. 1-flag
8. CHARLIE	38. OSCAR
9. MIKE	39. 3rd Sub.
10. SPEED	40. HOTEL
11. JULIETT	41. ECHO
12. 5-pennant	42. EMERG.
13. ROMEO	43. LIMA
14. 9-pennant	44. 7-pennant
15. ZULU	45. ϕ-flag
16. CORPEN	46. INT
17. 8-flag	47. DIV
18. UNIFORM	48. 4-pennant
19. 6-flag	49. 9-flag
20. X-RAY	50. 4th Sub.
21. NEGAT	51. PAPA
22. 2-flag	52. FORM
23. PORT	53. VICTOR
24. NOVEMBER	54. GOLF
25. 2-pennant	55. STARBOARD
26. TANGO	56. INDIA
27. 2nd Sub.	57. FOXTROT
28. BRAVO	58. QUEBEC
29. DELTA	59. 8-pennant
30. TURN	60. YANKEE
31. 5-flag	61. DESIG.
32. STATION	62. 7-flag
33. KILO	63. 3-pennant
34. 6-pennant	64. SQUADRON
35. WHISKEY	65. ANSWER
36. ϕ-pennant	

Then the sequence is started over again. On the *Eagle,* the procedure for rigging the rainbow is as follows:

2. Jackstaff to foremast: A block is set above the fore royal stay on the forward side of the mast; the halyard is secured at the foot of the jackstaff, and reeved through the block down to the fore crosstree; the

halyard is marked 150 feet from foot of the jackstaff; and the first twenty-five flags are bent on in accordance with the order listed above. The hooks are connected to the snap rings of the flags and are made free for running at the foot of the jackstaff.

3. Foremast to mainmast: The distance from the foretruck to maintruck is 88 feet and requires the next thirteen flags in order. Blocks are placed on the after side of foretruck and the forward side of maintruck. The halyard is reeved from the fore crosstree through the foretruck block to the maintruck block and down to the main cross-tree; the 13 flags are bent on and made up for running. The foremast to mainmast flags are set from the main cross-tree and are set taut from the fore cross-tree.

4. Mainmast to mizzenmast: The distance from the maintruck to mizzentruck is 68 feet and requires the next twelve flags in succession. Blocks are set, similar to those in "foremast to mainmast"; likewise, halyards are reeved and twelve flags are bent on free for running with this halyard and the flags stopped off on the main crosstree. The mainmast to mizzenmast flags are set from the mizzen top and are set taut from the main cross-tree.

5. Mizzenmast to flagstaff: The distance from the mizzenmast to flagstaff, at the level of awning, is 107 feet and requires the next nineteen flags in succession. The halyard is secured on the flagstaff at the point level with the awning and is reeved through a block, previously rigged on the after side of the mizzentruck, down to the mizzen top. The halyard is marked 107 feet from the flagstaff, and the nineteen flags

previously designated are bent on and laid out free for running on top of the awning.

Rigging Gear on Deck

Rigging and Operation of the Cargo Boom

The cargo boom was formerly used for launching and recovering small boats which were located in chocks on the gallows frame over the laundry. Since these boats have been removed, the boom is usually used only when loading or unloading heavy gear (figure 46).

There are four lines that must be rigged to operate the boom: the topping lift, two vangs, and the whip or hoist.

Figure 46. Cargo boom rigging.

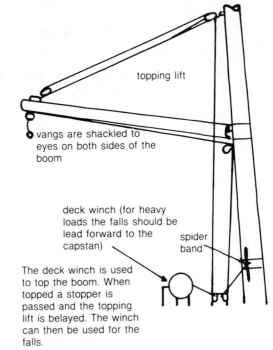

topping lift

vangs are shackled to eyes on both sides of the boom

deck winch (for heavy loads the falls should be lead forward to the capstan)

spider band

The deck winch is used to top the boom. When topped a stopper is passed and the topping lift is belayed. The winch can then be used for the falls.

1. The *topping lift* is used to adjust the height of the boom. The lift consists of a three-fold purchase which runs from an eye just below the main top to one at the head of the boom. When the boom is not being used, the topping lift is usually left shackled to the fitting on the mast; the block that attaches to the head of the boom is seized off out of the way at the foot of the mast or at the spider band. Thus, the first step in rigging the boom is to shackle the lower topping lift block to the head of the boom. The hauling end of the lift is led through a fairlead block at the base of the mast and then to the waist winch. When the boom is topped, the lift is secured to the cleat just below the spider band on the mast.

2. The *vangs* are used to control the athwartship motion of the boom. Unless an unusually heavy load is to be handled, gun tackles are shackled into the eyes on each side of the head of the boom. The lower end of the tackles are shackled to padeyes on deck. The choice of padeyes to use depends on the side on which the cargo is to be worked and on how far the boom must be swung. In general, the vangs should lead at as close to right angles from the boom as possible.

3. The *whip* or *hoist* is a purchase permanently rigged between the head and foot of the boom. When the boom is to be used, the hauling end of the purchase is run through a fairlead at the base of the mast to the winch. The hoist should be led to the opposite winch drum from the topping lift so that both lines can be worked together.

The operation of the boom is simple but requires great care to ensure safety. The boom is first topped by hauling on the topping lift purchase and easing the vangs. When topped, a stopper is passed and the purchase is belayed on the spider band. The boom is then centered over the load by means of the vangs, hauling on one and easing the other. The hoist is attached to the load and hauled up by the winch. The load should be lifted only to the height necessary to clear obstructions. When swinging the boom with a load, the cadets handling the vangs must be extremely careful in case the load swings out of control. Thus, close coordination is needed between the personnel working each vang. All loads should be rigged with tag (steadying) lines to prevent them from swinging out of control.

Rigging the Accommodation Ladder

The accommodation ladder consists essentially of an upper and lower platform, connected by a ladder as shown in figure 47. The lower end of the ladder, which has been connected to the lower platform, is held in place by a chain bridle with a bail and, from the bail, a chain ladder which shackles to a fishplate on the davit. The lower platform is equipped with leather fenders to protect boats from being damaged when coming alongside.

The following items are required prior to rigging: 2-yard tackles, tag lines, manila and wire straps, jigger, 3 snatchblocks, and wrenches and marlinspikes.

The procedure for rigging the accommodation ladder is not difficult. Due to the weight and cumbersome size, however, it is imperative that the initial rigging (such as yard tackles and straps) be done properly. If the *Eagle* is under sail, all main sails have

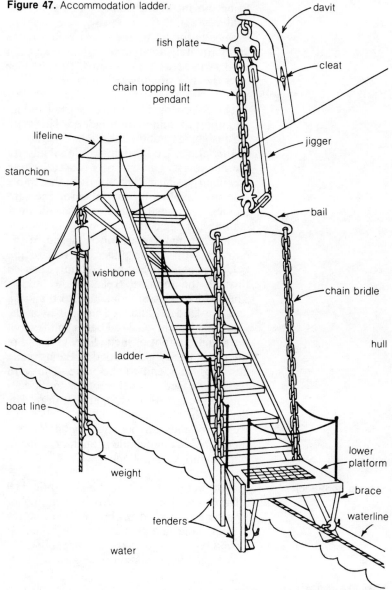

Figure 47. Accommodation ladder.

to be put in their gear prior to rigging the ladder.

Rigging the accommodation ladder takes approximately an hour and a half. The main yard is used as a boom to lift the ladder over the side and lower it into position.

The following procedure is used in rigging the accommodation ladder. The main yard is squared and all sections and fittings of the ladder are brought to the vicinity of the mainmast. One strap is passed around the main yardarm directly over the ship's side and the other further inboard. The yard tackles are rigged to the straps with their hauling parts led through snatchblocks on deck. The upper platform is rigged to the bulwark with toggle pins. The rest of the ladder is assembled and a strap is passed through the topmost tread of the ladder. The yard tackles are shackled to the strap and the ladder is hoisted up and over the side. The jigger is hooked between the davit head and the foot of the ladder. One end of the chain leader is shackled to the fishplate and the other end to the yoke. The yard tackle is eased until the top of the ladder can be secured to the upper platform. The jigger is then lowered until the bail takes the weight of the ladder. The rigging is completed by installing the stanchions, handrails, manropes, and guest warp.

Rigging Boat Booms

Boat booms allow small boats to tie well clear of the sides of vessels lying at anchor or moored to a mooring buoy. The order for a boat alongside to tie up to a boom is: *"Haul out to the port (starboard) boom."*

A boat boom (shown in Figure 48) con-

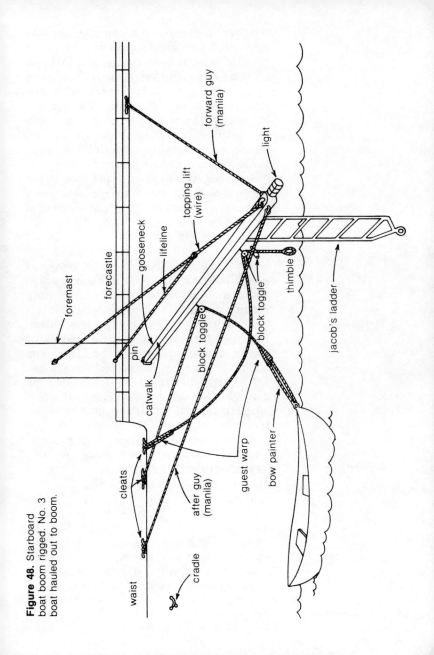

Figure 48. Starboard boat boom rigged. No. 3 boat hauled out to boom.

sists of a stout spar secured by its gooseneck (inboard end fitting) to a pin in the side, which allows free motion fore and aft in a horizontal plane. The outboard end of the boom hangs from a topping lift which is a single wire with chain length in the lower end. The topping lift keeps the boom constantly at the proper height. Fore-and-aft motion of the boom is controlled by lines called forward and after guys.

A strong two-inch or three-inch nylon line called a "guest warp" leads from a forward point on the ship out through a block at the outboard end of the boom. The outboard end of the guest warp is spliced around a metal thimble through which boats reeve their bow lines. A toggle is seized between strands of the guest warp, above the thimble to keep the latter from running up out of reach when a boat lets it go. One or more "Jacob's Ladders" hanging from the boom make it possible for boats' crews to get aboard the *Eagle*. The lifeline is made from a two-inch manila line and is approximately three feet above the catwalk. One end is made fast to the topping lift; the other end is secured to ship's railing or stanchion.

Rigging out the boom is a simple process. The boom stows in a chock alongside, with its outboard end aft. Ladder, guys, topping lift, and guest warps are attached. The guys lead out fore and aft with slack coiled down free for running. A two-fold purchase is hooked to a padeye on deck and to the topping lift. The boom is topped up to clear the chock. The boom is started out with a shove from a boat hook and the forward guy is hauled hard until the after one comes taut. This initial push is important since the boom has to travel three or four feet in order for the forward guy to be able to haul the boom out perpendicular to the hull. It takes from five to ten men to haul the boom out with the forward guy.

A boat is always made fast to a guest warp by the bight of its bow line, with the end secured back in the boat. This allows for quick release. The boat always rides to a long lead on the bow line. The shorter the lead, the more vertical the strain, and the more of the boat's weight there is on the bow line as she rides up and down on swells. Boats at booms have parted their lines or pulled out cleats or padeyes because the leads on their bow lines were too short.

Every man traveling over a boat boom must wear a life jacket, use the life line, and exercise caution against falling.

In securing the boat boom, the boom is topped with the topping lift until the boom makes a 30° angle (approximately) with the horizon. The forward guy is eased handsomely. The boom is always below the gunwale as it comes in, and a fender is available to absorb shock as the boom comes alongside.

The *Eagle* has a short single boat boom to port and a long double boat boom to starboard.

CONDITIONS OF CLOSURE: WATERTIGHT INTEGRITY

Buoyancy and stability are two essential attributes of any ship; they must be preserved if she is to continue to float and to sail. Numerous compartments with watertight boundaries and proper distribution of weight give the vessel buoyancy and stability.

Leakage of water into a compartment that is designed to be dry will diminish buoyancy. It is likely to have an adverse effect upon stability by introducing weight at the wrong place. Therefore, a prime objective in ship construction is watertight boundaries. Ideally, all boundary surfaces would be continuous with no possible sources of leakage: no doors, hatches, portholes, vent ducts or cable runs through bulkheads. However, there must be access, and habitability demands ventilation. So designers have to compromise between watertight construction and usability. They cut the watertight boundaries to provide the necessary access.

Still, the ship must be capable of being made watertight in the event of situations such as collision or grounding. Water that might accidentally enter the hull must be prevented from flooding progressively from one compartment to the next. In order to retain watertightness in boundaries containing openings, each fitting is provided with a watertight closure.

If all fittings were closed, the ship would be watertight. There would be no access, however. It would be possible to maintain a high degree of watertightness or watertight integrity if only one door were to be opened, with a man posted to close it again immediately, if necessary. A relatively high degree of watertight integrity would be maintained if only a few fittings were to be opened under these same circumstances.

Each such opening would reduce the

total watertight integrity somewhat. To have knowledge of the extent to which it has been diminished, there must be a record of what fittings are open. The watertight integrity maintained in a vessel such as the *Eagle* at a particular time is called its *material condition*.

While this procedure maintains good control over watertightness, it is more restrictive than is needed during the working day in fair weather. Under these circumstances, it is reasonable to keep frequently used access doors open at all times. Personnel are up and about and are close enough to the fittings to close them promptly in case of accident. On the other hand, when everyone is turned in at night, it may be unnecessary and imprudent to leave a particular door open.

There are three different standard material conditions which may be prescribed for the *Eagle*, depending upon the degree of watertight integrity that must be maintained.

These are:

1. *Material Condition X-Ray:* the most relaxed condition. Suitable for fair weather, daytime, and in port.

2. *Material Condition Yoke:* an intermediate condition used at night, in heavy weather, and when in restricted waters.

3. *Material Condition Zebra:* the most secure material condition in which the ship can continue to operate. Suitable for extremely foul weather, attack, or when damage is imminent.

4. A fourth intermediate state of readiness is *Yoke (Modified)*. When this is authorized, certain often-used *Yoke* fittings

may be left open without specific authorization by the officer of the deck. The fittings which may be left open are listed in the Damage Control Closure Log.

In order to determine what fittings are to be open or closed in each of the material conditions, each closure is classified according to its function and importance. A letter (X, Y, Z, or W) indicating the classification is attached to each fitting and the following closure table is applied:

Material Condition	Classification			
	X	Y	Z	W
X-Ray	Closed	Open	Open	Open
Yoke	Closed	Closed	Open	Open
Zebra	Closed	Closed	Closed	Open

A label with a circle around it is designated as *circle x-ray (yoke, zebra)*. This label indicates that the fitting (usually hatches and watertight doors) may be opened for passage without obtaining permission from the officer of the deck as long as the fitting is immediately secured again.

Whenever it becomes necessary to open a fitting which is supposed to be closed according to the material condition in effect, permission must be obtained from the officer of the deck. When requesting permission, cadets must give the name and rank/rate of the person making the request, the type of fitting, the number of the fitting, the classification of the fitting, and the reason for the request.

When permission is given to open, this information is logged with the time in the Closure Log. The closure of a fitting is reported promptly. This is also logged.

Glossary

Note: Terms enclosed by quotation marks are used as commands.

aback: A sail is aback when the wind strikes it on the opposite side from the normal situation: can be done on purpose in maneuvering or can happen accidentally.

after steering: The emergency steering station which is manned if there is a casualty to the main steering station on the bridge. On the *Eagle*, after steering is located on the fantail.

anemometer: An instrument used to measure the direction and speed of the wind. The sensor for the anemometer is located on the mizzen mast. *Eagle*'s instrument gives the relative wind direction and speed.

"Avast": Stop executing last command and hold what you have. Do not belay until directed.

backstay: Standing rigging leading from a point on the mast to the rail abaft the mast.

barque: A sailing vessel of three or more masts and whose after mast is fore-and-aft rigged. NOTE: The *Eagle* is *not* a ship. It is called one only for convenience in this manual. A ship is square-rigged on all masts.

belay: Secure the line to the belaying pin, cleat, or other point established for the purpose.

bend: To fasten a sail securely to the jackstay on a yard by means of robbands.

blanket: A sail is blanketed when the wind

is prevented from striking it either by another ship passing close aboard to weather or by the sails on another mast.

"Board the tack": Hook a special tackle [tay-kul] called the "tack jigger" in the weather clew of the foresail or mainsail and haul it down to the rail. Used when sailing close-hauled.

bobstay: A heavy stay (a steel rod on *Eagle*) running from the stem to the bowsprit.

boltrope: Roping around the edges of a sail.

boom: (1) The spar used to support the foot of the spanker. (2) A spar used to extend the reach of a line for handling cargo or in mooring boats, as in the cargo boom and boat boom.

bowsprit: The large spar standing from the bow of a sailing vessel. Provides a good lead for the stays which support the mast.

boxing: A maneuver that can be used when the *Eagle* has missed stays or has been taken aback. The fore yards are kept aback and, as the vessel loses headway, the bow pays off rapidly to leeward, at which point the maneuver of wearing ship may be carried through.

brace in: To swing the yards more athwartships or perpendicular to the keel.

braces: Running rigging used to swing the yards in a horizontal plane.

brails: Lines used to bring the spanker in to the mast while furling.

broach: To be thrown by wind or seas broadside to the seas and in their trough.

bull's-eye: A round or oval wooden block without a sheave. It has a groove around it for the strap and a hole for the lead of a line.

bumpkins: Metal poles supported by chains extending from the sides of the ship to support the blocks for the braces and to lead them clear of the side.

buntlines: Lines used to furl a square sail and bring the foot up to the yard.

bunt-leechlines: Lines on the royals and topgallant sails used to furl the square sails by bringing the leech and foot up to the yard.

cap: The top covering of the lower masts. In older sailing vessels the cap held the lower part of the topmasts to the lower masts.

cast or casting: To swing the vessel's head as necessary for getting underway.

catenary: A dip in a line caused by easing or slacking.

caught aback: The ship is caught aback when, due to a wind shift or helmsman error, the wind strikes the front rather than the back of the square sails.

chapell: A recovery maneuver used when caught aback: the main yards are squared, the stern is backed into the wind, and the ship is wore around.

"Clear away": Lay out a coil so that the line will run freely. Applies to downhauls, weather staysail sheets, etc.

"Clew down": Haul on the clewlines while holding the sheets in order to settle a yard.

clew garnets: Special term for the clewlines of the foresail and mainsail (courses).

clewlines: Lines leading to the lower corners of a square-sail, which bring them up to the yardarms when furling.

clew up: To bring the sail up in its gear by slacking sheets and hauling clewlines, buntlines, leechlines, and bunt-leechlines.

cockbill: Yards are cockbilled when they

are canted with respect to the horizontal. When sails are furled, the upper yards will cockbill when braced up. When sails are set, cockbill is adjusted by the fore and main lifts.

collision alarm: An alarm consisting of a series of short beeps indicating an imminent collision or grounding.

come-a-long: A chain or wire tackle with a ratchet mechanism used to lift or take a strain as the ratchet is engaged.

course: 1) Alternate term for the mainsail or foresail; 2) the intended heading of the vessel.

crane lines: Athwartship cables for men to work between the shrouds—similar to ratlines.

cringle: Iron ring in the boltrope of a sail at the head, clew or leech.

cross-trees: Athwartship members located where the topmast and topgallant mast come together.

deadman: An improperly furled section of a sail which looks as if a "dead man could be furled inside it."

dead reckoning tracer: A device located in the Combat Information Center (CIC) which combines course and speed information to give a visual record of the ship's dead (deduced) reckoning plot.

dolphin striker: A strut or brace extending almost vertically from the bowsprit to the bobstay.

douse: To take in a sail.

downhaul: Line leading to the deck from the head of a staysail for hauling it down.

earring: A short piece of line secured to a

cringle. Used for hauling out the head of a square sail when bending it on the yard.

"Ease": Pay out slowly and with care; reduce strain on the line. Used for halyards, etc.

fairlead: A block or fitting which changes the direction (lead) of a line without giving mechanical advantage or which allows it to run without chafing (fair).

falls: The line in a tackle, which is roven through the blocks to create a mechanical advantage.

fid: A tapered wooden rod normally used in splicing line but also used to secure the sea painter on the small boats and, in a steel version, to support the topmasts when they are in the fully rigged position.

fiferail: A rail around three sides of each mast used to hold belaying pins for various running rigging.

flukes: The broad, triangular, flat sections of the anchor which actually dig into the bottom. The flukes can rotate on the anchor stock. Occasionally, when the anchor is weighed, the flukes will point in toward the hull and will have to be "tripped" or rotated so that they face outwards.

full and by: Sailing close to the wind with the sails drawing full and conforming to the changes in direction of the wind.

furl: To take in a sail and secure it.

gaff: A spar on the mizzen used for extending the head of the spanker.

gantline: A whip (purchase) rigged aloft for general utility purposes.

gasket: Line or canvas strap used to secure a sail when furled.

goosewing: To set only the lee half of a sail. Chafing gear is passed around the sail at the center of the yard and the weather side remains furled or in its gear. The mainsail may be goosewinged to allow wind through to the foresails when sailing with the wind aft of the quarter.

halyard: Running rigging for hoisting and lowering sails and yards.

"Hand over hand": Face towards the point of pull (opposite the direction of pull) and pull first with one hand and then the other.

hank: Circular metal fitting which rides on a stay and to which the luff of a staysail is seized.

head: The top edge of a square sail which is bent to the yard.

headreach: The distance the ship moves forward before stopping when the engines are stopped, sails doused, or the ship heads into the wind as in tacking. The concept is analogous to the advance in a turn.

"Heave around": To haul on a line by machinery. Since this is very seldom the case on the *Eagle*, the command does not deserve its present vogue. The proper command is "Haul," or one of its variations.

heave to (under sail): To kill the ship's headway by turning into the wind or by backing the yards on one or more masts.

heavy weather bill: A procedure which readies the ship for riding out a storm. The bill requires rigging life lines, lashing down loose gear, and setting maximum conditions of material and engineering readiness.

helm indicator: A dial located on the helm stand which indicates how many degrees the helm has been turned. The steering indicator, located in the pilot house, shows how many degrees the rudder has actually moved.

in extremis: A ship is *in extremis* when only immediate action by both vessels is sufficient to avoid collision.

inhaul: Line used to haul in the head or foot of the spanker.

in irons: A ship is in irons when it stops during a tack with the wind dead ahead and cannot be turned either way.

in its gear: When a sail has been drawn up and is being held by its gear: buntlines, leechlines, bunt-leechlines and clewlines.

in its lifts: A yard is in its lifts when the halyard has been slacked off and the yard pulled down so that its entire weight is supported by the lifts.

jackstay: A metal rod to which sails or lines are fastened.

jibe: A jibe occurs when the ship turns to bring the wind across the stern. In a square-rigger a jibe implies that the shift of the wind was unintentional. If intentional, "wear" is used.

jigger: A handy purchase (tackle), generally used to take additional strain on running rigging.

knock down: The ship is knocked down when the wind heels it over beyond its limit of stability so that it cannot return to the vertical.

leather: A short strip of leather tucked into the braces after they have stretched out to mark when the yards are braced square or sharp.

lee: The side away from the wind.

leech: The after edge of a fore-and-aft sail; the sides of a square sail.

leechlines: Lines leading to the sides of a square sail which bring them up to the yardarms when furling.

"Let go and haul": Swing the yards of the foremast to the opposite tack when maneuvering under sail.

lift: Used to indicate that the square sails are luffing; that is, that the wind is striking along the leeches, causing them to shake rather than fill.

lifts: Standing lifts are rigged on royal, topgallant, and upper topsail yards to keep them level when fully lowered. Running lifts are rigged on the fore and main yards to permit canting of all the yards (with sails set) as required.

lizard: A short length of line having a thimble (or thimbles) spliced into its ends. Used as a leader for rigging.

luff: The forward edge of a fore-and-aft sail; the shake or slat of a sail when the sheet is too slack or the vessel too close to the wind.

"Mainsail haul": Swing the yards of the mainmast to the opposite tack when maneuvering under sail.

marry: To twist together a standing line and a running line so that the friction between the two will prevent the running line from running free. Lines are married in order to allow the running line to be belayed.

masthead: The top of a lower mast where foretop or maintop is situated.

"Man": Station sufficient men to haul on the line against the anticipated strain.

miter seam: The seam of a headsail or

staysail which leads from the clew to the center of the luff and at which the panels, which run parallel to the foot and the leech, meet.

on the wind: Close-hauled, or sailing as close to the wind as possible.

outhaul: Line used to haul out the head or the foot of the spanker.

"Overhaul": Assist in rendering freely. Applies to extending a tackle, pulling up slack in buntlines, etc.

padeye: A ring or eye welded to the deck to which blocks may be shackled.

peak: The outermost upper corner of the spanker or any sail bent to a gaff; the uppermost corner of a triangular sail where the luff and leech meet.

pendant: A short piece of line or wire with an eye at each end. Used for hanging off a block, footrope, etc.

pole: The upper end of the highest mast, between the royal yard and the truck.

pooped: A ship is pooped when seas break over its stern.

preventer: A line or tackle used to provide extra safety. The most common preventer on the *Eagle* is used to prevent the spanker boom from jibing.

rattail jigger: A light purchase with a stopper shackled to the becket of one block. Used to sweat down lines by passing the stopper around the line and hauling it down to deck.

"Rise tacks and sheets": Clew up the mainsail when maneuvering under sail.

roband: Short length of marlin used to secure the head of a square sail to the jackstay or the luff of a headsail to the hanks.

rotten stuff: Any of a variety of small yarns, usually salvaged from old lines, used to stop off gear. Rotten stuff must be strong enough to hold the gear but light enough to break easily when tugged.

"Round in": Bring the blocks of a tackle together by hauling on the line.

"Run away with": Face in the direction of pull, grasp the line with both hands, and run.

running rigging: Moveable lines and blocks used for controlling sails, yards, etc.

safety stay: The aftermost of the two jackstays on each yard. It is so called because it provides a hand hold (and a point of attachment for safety belt hooks) for personnel working on the yards.

scallops: Slack sections of the luff of a sail between the hanks. Scallops create turbulence and should be removed by hauling on the halyard.

scud: To run before the wind in heavy weather with reduced sail, such as the main lower topsail and the fore course.

seize: To fasten ropes together by turns of small stuff.

shaft alley: The compartment aft of the engine room through which the propellor shaft runs.

sheet: Running rigging secured to the clew of a sail (opposing a clewline).

"Sheet home": When setting the square sails, ease clewlines, buntlines, and leechlines, and haul on the sheets until only a few links of the sheet remain above the sheet block. Given to personnel on headsails and staysails to haul the sheets in and trim them to best advantage.

shoe: A fitting at the center of the upper three yards which rides in a track bolted to the mast and which is used to attach the yard to the mast.

shrouds: Standing rigging used to support a mast laterally, led athwartships from aloft to the rail.

"Slack": Pay out fairly rapidly; remove most of the strain from the line.

slot: The space between two headsails or staysails. The width of the slot should be adjusted by use of the sheets to create the fastest airflow, which will then increase the driving power of the sails.

small stuff: Small, light line designated by number of threads. Used for numerous odd purposes on a ship.

spider band: A metal band just above the bases of the masts, with fittings on which miscellaneous gear can be stowed.

spreader: Extension projecting horizontally at the cross-trees to spread backstays.

stacked: The yards are stacked when each is parallel to and aligned with the yard immediately below.

standing part: The fixed part of any piece of running rigging; the end which is secured permanently.

stays: (1) Standing rigging in line with the ship's keel; some stays carry staysails. (2) An alternate term for tacking. The ship is *in stays* while coming through the wind and *misses stays* when she does not make it through the wind.

step: Masts are stepped on (rest on) secure foundations on the keel or the lower decks.

stirrups: Wire rope pendants which are

seized to the jackstays and which are used to support the foot ropes.

tabling: A broad hem on the edge of sails used to give shape and strength to the sail. Replaces the boltrope of older sails.

tack: (1) A line leading forward from the clew of the foresail or mainsail. (2) The lower forward corner of a fore-and-aft sail.

tacking: A sailing maneuver: the process of bringing the ship's head through the wind to get the wind on the opposite side.

tack jigger: A tackle used to haul down the weather tack of foresail or mainsail.

"Tend": Station one man, or at most two, for the purpose of slacking or keeping the slack out of a line.

That's well: Command used to indicate that a line has been hauled enough. A milder form of *"Avast."*

throat: The forward upper corner of a fore-and-aft sail.

"Throw off": Take off pin and see that it runs freely. This never applies to lines under a heavy load, except in real emergencies. Used for buntlines when setting sail.

timenoguy: A line stretched from one point to another for the purpose of preventing gear from fouling; a piece of light line with a bull's eye spliced in the end. It supports long and heavy line like the main brace on the *Eagle*, which passes through the bull's-eye led from the mizzen shrouds.

top: (1) Platform at the top of a mast, as foretop or maintop, though not the actual uppermost point. (2) To haul on a topping lift to hoist either the cargo or spanker boom.

tophamper: The collective term for all yards, rigging, and gear above the deck.

topping lift: Purchase used for raising or taking the weight of a boom.

trick wheel: The emergency steering wheel located on the fantail on the *Eagle*.

"Trim": Adjust a sail by hauling in on the sheet (fore-and-aft sails) or brace.

truss: A U-shaped metal fitting secured to the center of the lower yards. A swivel at the outer end of the U connects the yard to the mast.

two-blocked (or chock-a-block): A purchase is two-blocked when the upper and lower blocks have been pulled together as far as possible. Used loosely for whips, signal halyards, and the like when the load (or flag) is hauled all the way up to the block.

tye: Part of the purchase used to raise the movable yards. On the *Eagle* it consists of a chain made fast to the center of the yard. The chain is led up through a sheave in the mast down to a fly block through which the halyard purchase is roven.

unfurl: To cast loose a sail by throwing off the gaskets.

vang: A line leading from the mizzen gaff to the deck to keep it steady when the spanker is not set (used in pairs on the *Eagle*).

wearing: A sailing maneuver: the process of bringing the ship's stern through the wind to get the wind on the opposite side.

weather: On the side toward the wind.

worm, parcel and serve: A method of protecting standing line. Worming is the process of filling the lays of a rope with small stuff wound spirally. Parceling consists of winding tarred canvas around a rope, while serving consists of winding small stuff tightly around a rope to hold the worming and parceling in position.

yard: A spar rigged horizontally on a mast, to which the head of a square sail is bent (made fast).